THE WESTERN ISLAND
OR
THE GREAT BLASKET

Rochelle—

with love

Miranda

Dingle, Aug '93

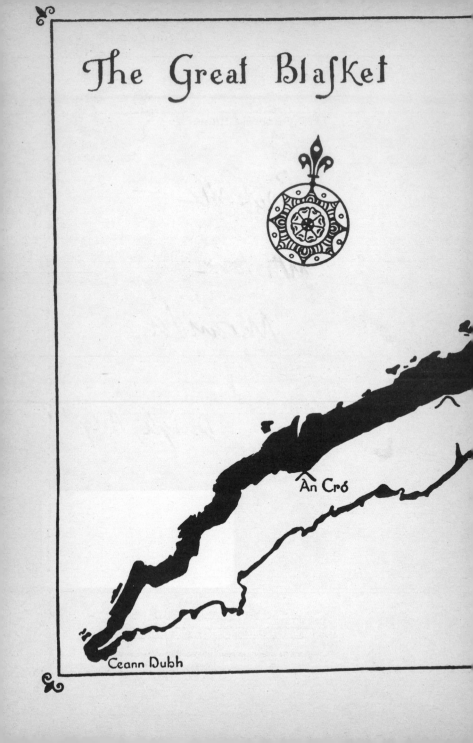

The Great Blasket

An Cró

Ceann Dubh

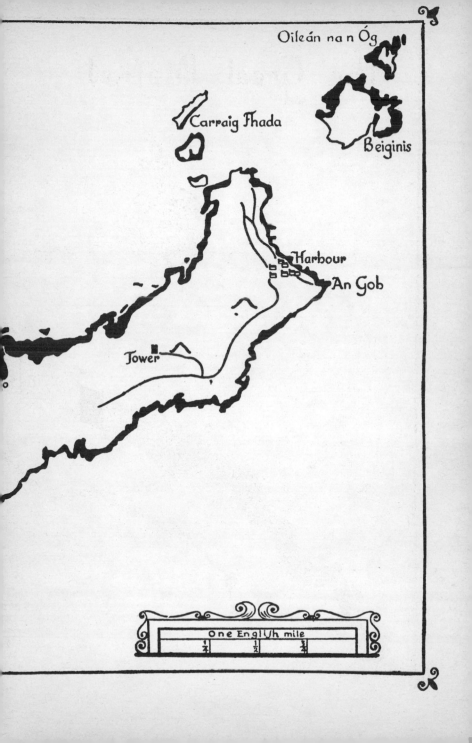

THE
WESTERN ISLAND
OR
THE GREAT BLASKET

By

ROBIN FLOWER

With illustrations
by
IDA M. FLOWER

Oxford   New York

OXFORD UNIVERSITY PRESS

Oxford University Press, Walton Street, Oxford OX2 6DP

Oxford New York Toronto
Delhi Bombay Calcutta Madras Karachi
Petaling Jaya Singapore Hong Kong Tokyo
Nairobi Dar es Salaam Cape Town
Melbourne Auckland

and associated companies in
Berlin Ibadan

First published 1944
Reprinted 1945, 1946, 1966, 1971, 1973
First issued as an Oxford University Press Paperback 1978
Reissued 1992

British Library Cataloguing in Publication Data
Flower, Robin
The western island; or, The Great Blasket.
1. Blasket Islands, Ire.—Social life
and customs
I. Title
941.9'6   DA990.B65   77–30566
ISBN 0–19–281234–3

Printed in Great Britain by
Clays Ltd,
Bungay, Suffolk

PREFACE

THIS book gives an account of my experiences during a number of intermittent holiday visits to the Great Blasket covering roughly a period of some twenty years. I first went to the Island in 1910, and my wife accompanied me there in the following year when she made the pen drawings from which the illustrations here have been reproduced. The text was written at various times in the course of the twenty years that followed. It was made the subject of part of a series of lectures on Irish literature delivered at the Lowell Institute in 1935, and I should like to take this opportunity (alas! too late) of returning my thanks to the late Laurence Lowell for the invitation to deliver these lectures and for his kindness to myself and my daughter while we were in Boston. The intercalated poems were written at the same time as the book, and are thus a product of the same experience. They were first published by Messrs. Constable in my book, *Poems and Translations*, in 1931, and I am grateful to them for their permission to reproduce them here in their original setting.

It will be immediately obvious to every reader how much I am indebted to three islanders—Tomás ó Crithin, Peig Sayers, and Gobnait Ní Chinéide. The first two are already well known to readers of Irish. Tomás's autobiography, *An t-Oileánach*, was published in 1929 and was translated into English by me from the original Irish under the title *The Islandman* in 1934. Peig's book, *Peig a sgéal féin*, 'Peig, her own story', was published in Irish in 1936 and met with immediate success. It has not been translated into English. But in addition to these three my gratitude is due to all the dwellers on the Island at the time of my visits. The population then consisted of upwards of 150 souls, now reduced, largely by emigration to the mainland, so that the very life of the Island in the form in which I knew it is threatened. On one of my visits after a long interval I remember how, on the evening of my return, a number of my friends had gathered in one of the houses to bid me welcome. In the course of our talk we began to reckon up the deaths which had occurred since my last visit. The talk inevitably took the form of a recitation of the rich store of proverbs accumulated in a folk civilization on the necessity of death and the consolations of religious faith. One by one, almost as though reciting a liturgy, men and women produced each one his or her contribution from that apparently inexhaustible supply. At last, however, a silence fell as they waited, visibly searching their minds for a fresh inspiration. Suddenly, an old woman in the corner leaned forward and said with an air of finality:

'Cá'il an sneachta bhí comh geal anuirig?' (Where is the snow that was so bright last year?)

I sprang up in excitement and cried out: 'Où sont les neiges d'antan?'

'Who said that?' asked the King, an expert in this lore.

'François Villon said it', I replied.

'And who was he?' he returned. 'Was he a Connaughtman?'

'No, he lived hundreds of years ago and he said it in French, and it was a proverb of his people.'

'Well,' broke in Tomás, 'You can't better the proverb. I've always heard that the French are a clever people, and I wouldn't put it past them to have said that before we did.'

The King is dead and Tomás and the greater part of that lamenting company, and all this that follows is the song we made together of the vanished snows of yesteryear.

R. F.

15 October 1944

CONTENTS

LIST OF ILLUSTRATIONS

MAPS

THE ROAD TO THE ISLAND

As the train passes through County Cork into County Kerry, going always farther and farther west, the changing country takes on more and more an aspect of barrenness. The woods, fields, and rich green water-meadows that gather round the great river of Blackwater are soon a fading memory; the hills begin to cluster on the horizon, and long melancholy stretches of bog-land are at last all the foreground and middle distance. We leave Killarney, which hides its lakes and woods from the traveller as a rich man his precious things from the casual wayfarer, and come at length to Tralee, the last station to the west on the line, and the door to the wild uplands of the Dingle peninsula. I have heard old people on the Blasket speak of a visit to Tralee as a Highlander might tell of Glasgow or a Warwickshire peasant of London. Dingle is their familiar home town, but Tralee is over the horizon, a place of seldom-seen wonders—the Court House with its derelict guns of ancient war, Donovan's Mills, and the great market-place where you may still hear the ballet-singers quavering out their endless songs to the rough accompaniment of the cattle.

To the little station of the Dingle line the country people come at the tail of a market-day with their motley purchases; you forget London and Dublin, all the cities of the earth, and with Gaelic faces and Gaelic voices about you stand in the gateway of an older and a simpler world. And when the last old woman with her last bundle has been safely taken on board, the train draws slowly out of the tiny station and idles along between the mountains and the sea to the junction for Castle Gregory. There it spills a tithe of its passengers and faces for the hills.

Gradually, past unfolding valleys, over bridges that span the tumbling mountain streams, along the steep sides of heather hills, it makes the ascent of the pass, leaving behind at last the long sweep of Tralee Bay and the shadowy heights beyond. You pass by Gleann na nGealt, where Suibhne Geilt and all the mad folk of Ireland came flying on the light wings of their ruined wits, and Gleann an Scáil, where Cúchulainn and the giant pelted one another with great rocks which, meeting in mid-course, crashed in numberless fragments to the valley below. Dingle Bay comes into sight, and the place where Aogán Ó Rathaille listened sleeplessly to the sleepless wave of Duibhneacha. He is still a remembered poet in these parts. There is a story of him told in the islands which I have not come across elsewhere. He was benighted with a friend, says the tale, in a lonely place among the mountains, and, seeing a house, said they would rest the night there.

'We can't stay there,' said the friend.

'And why not?' said Aogán.

'Because,' said the other, 'the man of the house is a miser, and never yet gave any man the night inside.'

'We will go in,' said Aogán, 'nevertheless.'

They went in, and he didn't say as much as 'Sit down', or 'Get out'.

Aogán sat down by the fire, and his friend beside him.

'Now, wasn't it an odd thing the crow said to me?' said Aogán.

'Sure, the crow never said anything yet,' said the man of the house.

'Ah, but he did!' said Aogán. 'Didn't he say: Aogán, Aogán, Aogán Ó Rathaille!'

'Is it you, Aogán Ó Rathaille?' says the man, jumping up from his corner. 'A hundred thousand welcomes to you, and stay inside till day!'

At last the train with its dwindled company drags into Dingle station, and, taking a car, you jolt along the dirty street that runs by the quay front, over the bridge, and away into the open country. It is a ten-mile drive to Dunquin, whether you go round by Slea Head or over the mountain pass between Sliabh an Iolair and Cruach Mhárthain, and as you go the barrenness of the land increases. There is a grove of trees round the house, once Lord Ventry's, at Baile an Ghóilín. Look well at them, for you will see no trees more, save some solitary ash or thorn, till you come this way again. All else is naked field and dun bog, starred here and there with the snow-soft bog-cotton, or touched into brightness by the wasteful gold of ragwort. On the hill-side stunted gorse-bushes spread in yellow masses amid the purple of the heather. And here and there by the roadway fuchsias hang out their waxen pendants, looking oddly artificial in this wild landscape, like the incongruous finery a country girl puts on for a fair day. Gulls fly and scream over the bogs, and here and there a heron floats indolently, or perches one-legged in a shallow stream.

Across the bay the hills of Íbh Ráthach draw a ragged line along the sky, and on the other hand the country rises till the huge shape of Mount Brandon has nothing beyond it but clouds and blue air. The car rattles through Ventry, a straggle of houses lying back from the long strand where they hold horse-races now, but where in old tales and the country traditions Fionn and the Fenians still fight their unequal battles against Dáire Donn and the hosts of the world.

Out of Ventry the ascent begins, and the road climbs between the flat table-land of Sliabh an Iolair and the pointed crest of Cruach Mhárthain that has on its summit a cromlech, a *leaba Dhiarmada agus Gráinne*, where none the less the flying lovers never rested, but Diarmaid, says the tale, kept watch for Fionn over the harbour of Dingle. By the side of the road runs a deep and wide trench into which, they say, a drunkard once fell with his ass-cart, and lay there dead, man and ass, for a week before men found them. With this tale in my mind I once drove over this pass in the falling night with a drunken driver and a girl muttering prayers, and I thought the poor drunkard stirred uneasily in his sleep expecting company for his loneliness.

From the top of the pass you look back and see a world of bog and mountain and sea stretching far behind you. Of this pass the islanders tell the tale, so common throughout Ireland, of the woman who had never stirred from her home, and on her first venture, coming to the crest of the pass and gazing over the spreading landscape, cried out: 'What a wide, weary place is Ireland!' and, frightened by the vastness of the revealed world, turned back for ever to her cosy, familiar island.

A little farther along the road the other view breaks on you—the sea and the islands and the far Atlantic horizon. Below is Dunquin, whitewashed houses here and there and a pattern of fields along the hill-side. Then the cliff breaks to the sea, and three miles out lie the islands. They are the peaks of hills sundered from their mainland brothers, and seen thus from above you would think them sea-monsters of an antique world languidly lifting time-worn backs above the restless and transitory waves. Nearest to us is Beiginis, a small flat island of good grass, with a youngling island, Oileán na nÓg, lying under its flank. Beyond it the Great Blasket, An t-Oileán Mór, rises to its high central hill, screening from view the two smaller islands, Inis na Bró and Inisicíleáin. To the right is the Northern Island, Inis Tuaisceart, ending in a curious serrated crag which the islanders liken vividly to a cockscomb. Far out in the sea soars the gull-haunted pyramid of the Tiaracht, which carries the last light that

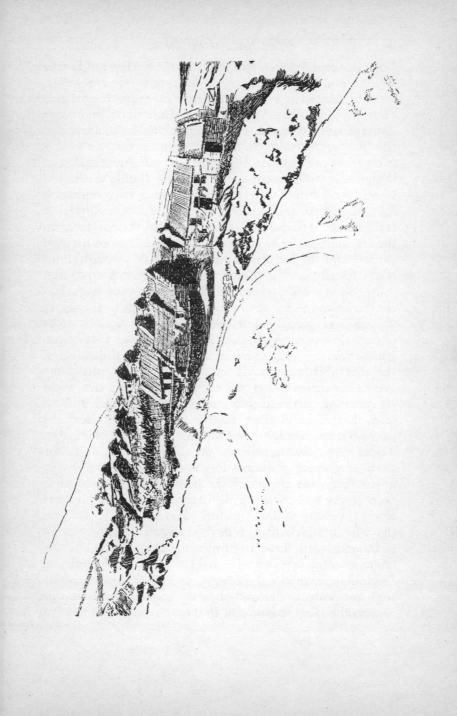

Irish emigrants see as they go on their long voyage to America. For this is the ultimate shore of the old world, the islands are the westernmost of all the inhabited lands of Europe, and until the time of Columbus there was nothing beyond but the waste sea. 'Wasn't it a great thought Columbus had', said a man to me once as we lay gazing out over the Atlantic, 'to find out America? For if there wasn't America, the Island wouldn't stand a week'. And this is true, for that growing barrenness has here reached its term, and only perhaps in those parts of Ireland where the soil has to be made on the rocks before the scant crop can be sown will you find a more niggard earth. And the harvest of the sea and the contributions of the American exiles alone maintain life on the Island.

As you descend the cliff at Dunquin to take boat, you see the jagged edges of the rocks leaning out to the sea as though in a perpetual defence against the furious onset of the waves. A rough path down the steep cliff brings you to the slip, and there, rocking lightly on the water, the boat waits for you. These boats, the curraghs of the West, are here called *naomhóga*. They are the usual structure of lath framework and tarred canvas, and no craft in the world rides more lightly on the water, or answers more readily to the faintest suggestion of the oar. There is no greater pleasure on earth than to lie in the stern of a *naomhóg*, almost in the embrace of the water, as the strong rowers snatch the boat over the waves. The boat works out of the little harbour and sets a course along the shore under the cliffs. Here from the sea-level the Island, which had seemed so near from the summit of the cliff, withdraws itself into the distance behind the dancing company of the waves. 'Say your farewell to Ireland', cries one of the rowers, and I turn and bid farewell, not only to Ireland, but to England and Europe and all the tangled world of to-day.

THE PASSAGE

THE boat runs rapidly over the waves to the hasty rhythm of the six short, almost bladeless oars; or, if the wind is fair, following the pull of the tiny, patched sail. You see the coast going by, and the blunt headland of Dún Mór, once the home of a fabled goddess, with a rock at its end, An Seanduine, the Old Man, a familiar seamark to the islanders. Then the lifting prow turns to the Island, and in a short while the boat is running by Beiginis, and the high front of the Island begins to rise over you. To the right is a long shore of sand, An Tráigh Bhán, the White Strand, and in front a flat reef of rock, anvil-shaped, shuts in the tiny harbour. The boat runs in, turns on its axis, and you are floating easily up to the slip, under a great cliff fringed with children perilously running on its dizzy brink. The passage is over, and it has been an easy one. But there are days, sometimes even weeks, when the Island is shut off from the outside world by the anger of the sea. There is an odd tale of one such winter isolation in the old time which may well be told here. This is how I heard it from the story-teller:

'In those days there was no priest nearer the Island than Paróiste Múrach. A family on the Island had a baby, and they were waiting to sail from day to day, but it was heavy weather in the depth of winter, and maybe they were not too set on going, anyhow. So the child was left unbaptized for a year and a day. Then at long last they made ready, and there was a boat going to Dingle by sea; they got into it, father, mother, and child, and the baby was just beginning to walk. When they reached the priest's house he had gone off with him somewhere, so the woman of the house told the wife to sit down, and the baby began to yell. The woman of the house said there was something ailing him.

' "Not it," said the wife. "He's always like that when he hasn't got an egg in his hand."

' "Why," says the woman of the house, "you must be a bit childish yourself if you think that raw babe could keep an egg in his hand."

' "Indeed and on my mantle," says the mother, "he could that, and eat it too."

' "Do you tell me," says the woman, "that a child not yet baptized could eat an egg?"

' "I do," says the woman.

' "Is he well-grown?" says the other.

' "Well, maybe he's close on a month old," says she.

' "Is a child not a month old able to hold an egg in his hand and eat it too?" says the woman.

' "He would," says the mother, "if there was any stuff in it."

' "Where do you come from?"

' "From the Island, my friend."

' "It's little wonder the people there are wild," says the woman, "for they're wild in their mother's womb. Have you breast-milk enough for him?"

' "Not a drop," says the mother, "nor I don't need it neither."

' "What do you give him to eat and drink, then?"

' "A fresh egg, a bit of fresh fish, a piece of fresh rabbit, and every mouthful I have he has his share of it."

' "O glory be to God!" says the woman of the house.

'It wasn't long till the priest came in, and the woman said to him that she had a baby for baptism.

' "Where's he from?" says the priest.

' "From the Western Island," says she.

' "What brought him here?" says he.

' "They came right through the bay," says she.

' "It's a marvel they didn't lose the child and they so long on the sea," says he.

' "Long as they were," says she, "he didn't mind it, for every baby they have there walks by the month's end."

' "What do you say?" says he.

' "That's what I say," says she, "and this one's walking and he isn't a month yet."

' "Tell the mother I want her."

'The mother came.

' "Where are you from?"

' "From the Island, father."

' "Is that a baby for baptism you have there?"

' "It is, father."

' "How old is he?"

' "Hardly a month yet."

' "Didn't the woman tell me he was walking?"

' "He's beginning at it, father."

' "And him not a month yet?"

' "Yes and indeed, father," says she.

' "Have you any other children?"

' "Yes, father, six more."

' "Did any other of them start to walk as soon as this one?"

' "Yes, father, all of them. This one makes the worst show of them all at it."

'The priest was thunderstruck when he heard this, and he stood thinking a while.

' "Does every baby on the Island begin to walk as soon as that?" says he.

' "Yes, and sooner too, some of them."

'He stopped again for a bit.

' "Is that an egg in his hand?" says he.

' "Yes, it is," says she, "I told the woman to boil it long ago, for the poor thing's hungry."

' "Do you tell me he'd eat it if it was boiled?"

' "He would, by my mantle," says she, "for he'd have had three of them down him since morning if he'd been at home."

' "Well," says the priest, "the like of that tale I never heard yet. We may as well baptize him," says he, "perhaps you're hungry as well as the baby."

'He told the woman to take the egg from him for a while, and she did so and you could hear him yelling all over Dingle. They had to give it back to him, and he kept hold of it all the time the baptism was going on. When he was baptized the priest said: "If he lives," says he, "he will be like the Fenians of Ireland. Get plenty to eat for yourself and the baby from the housekeeper."

' "Your health, father," says she.

'The baby's alive still, he had strong enough bones, but, believe me, he was far enough from the strength of the Fenians. I give you my word, the island woman was no fool; they thought they had the laugh of her, but 'tis she that had the laugh of them.'

You might well believe, to see the babies running on the cliff above the harbour, that they had all walked before a month's end. They scream out as the boat slides up to the slip, and all stand eagerly gazing while the men unload and then, lifting the boat out of the water and getting underneath it, walk up the path like a six-legged black-beetle. They stow it away on a trestle, and then we all climb to the top of the cliff. We have reached the Island.

We have come in on the post-boat. The big, heavy man, with the broad, benignant face and the easy, authoritative air as of the captain of a coasting schooner, who leads the way up the path, carries a bag slung over his shoulder. He is the King of the Island, Pádraig Ó Catháin, the diplomatist and chief man of authority in the village,

who holds his office by sheer weight of character. He
halts on the broad space at the top of the cliff, unslings
and opens his bag, and the children gather excitedly
round him while he perches a pair of spectacles on his
nose and, taking out the letters one by one, reads the
addresses aloud. As each address is read a child puts out
an eager hand and runs off with the letter to its destina-
tion. When all the letters are gone, and all the crowd
dispersed, we move on up the village.

Thus the news of the outer world comes to the Island;
from the mainland, from the next parish, which is
America, and from England, which spiritually is so much
farther away. I remember, in a fatal year, how I stood
watching the little sail of the post-boat flitting across the
Sound, and went with the children to await its arrival.
The King came slowly up the slope with his bag, set it
down on the ground, and, turning to me, said with a
grave air: 'There is news to-day. They have killed an
Archduke in the eastern world.' It meant little to us then
in that remote isolation of the sea; but in a month's time
I was back in London, and the familiar fabric of life was
torn like a cobweb in the wind for all of us—and, though
the revelation came later, for the Island also. In a few
years' time their bay was full of anti-submarine craft, and
the tide was bringing the wreckage of ships and the quiet
forms of the dead to the Island beaches. But this was for
the future when first I knew the Island, and these are not
the memories which I cherish most willingly.

As we climb the path running under the steep face of
the hill the village unfolds beneath us: an irregular
huddle of houses crouching down out of the wind wherever
a bank can be found for shelter, and showing to the sky
black tarred roofs on which the flattened forms of fish are
drying. At the top of the village is the well where women
and children wait with buckets and cans while the earth

slowly gives out its cherished water. An ass stands by
with lowered head, waiting patiently under the load of
his panniers brimming with brown turf; and an incessant
chattering goes on as the water-carriers playfully wrangle
for precedence, or pass from mouth to mouth the constant
excited gossip of lonely country places. They call out to
us as we go by, and we exchange greetings with them,
recognizing old friends and renewing an old acquaintance.
Then we enter the King's kitchen, he sets down his bag,
and in formal and eloquent words welcomes us back to
the Island. We are happy to be here again, and, as friend
following friend comes forward to greet us, it is as though
from a long absence we were at last home once more.

In Dingle we have provided ourselves with a large can
of mixed sweets, and as the news spreads through the
houses, there is an instantaneous mobilization of the
infantry. The kitchen fills at a rush with wild-haired
children, the whole mass swaying with an odd movement
which is a curious mixture of thrusting forward and
drawing back, of boldness and modesty, of good manners
and eagerness. The King's daughter marshals the
irregular forces and, one by one, they shuffle forward and
retire, each happy with a handful of sweets. The kitchen
gradually empties as they run out on to the hill to gloat
over their prize. But a sudden feeling comes upon you of
a new presence in the room. You look up and see, leaning
against the wall almost with the air of a being magically
materialized out of nothing, a slight but confident figure.
The face takes your attention at once and holds it. This
face is dark and thin, and there look out of it two quick
and living eyes, the vivid witnesses of a fine and self-
sufficing intelligence. He comes towards you, and with a
grave and courteous intonation, and a picked and running
phrase, bids you welcome. You have indeed come home, for
this is Tomás Ó Crithin, the Island poet and story-teller.

The Passage at Night

THE dark cliff towered up to the stars that flickered
And seemed no more than lights upon its brow,
And on the slippery quay
Men talked—a rush of Gaelic never-ending.
I stepped down to the boat,
A frail skin rocking on the unquiet water,
And at a touch she trembled
And skimmed out lightly to the moonlit seaway.
I lying in the stern
Felt all the tremble of water slipping under,
As wave on wave lifted and let us down.
The water from the oars dripped fiery; burning
With a dull glow great globes
Followed the travelling blades. A voice rose singing
To the tune of the running water and loud oars:
'I met a maiden in the misty morning,
And she barefooted under rippling tresses.
I asked her was she Helen, was she Deirdre?
She answered: "I am none of these, but Ireland.
Men have died for me, men have still to die." '
The voice died then, and, growing in the darkness,
The shape of the Great Island
Rose up out of the water hugely glooming,
And wearing lights like stars upon its brow.

Tomás

I LOITERED there, and he
Built up the turf-rick with how careful hands;
Hands that had built a thousand ricks and now
Worked delicately with a deft unconsciousness.
Below us the Great Island
Fell with white-shining grasses to the cliffs,
And there plunged suddenly
Down sheer rock-gullies to the muttering waves.
Far out in the bay the gannets
Stopped and turned over and shot arrowy down,
And, beyond island, bay, and gannets falling,
Ireland, a naked rock-wave, rose and fell.
He had lived on the Island sixty years
And those years and the Island lived in him,
Graved on his flesh, in his eye dwelling,
And moulding all his speech,
That speech witty and beautiful
And charged with the memory of so many dead.
Lighting his pipe he turned,
Looked at the bay and bent to me and said:
'If you went all the coasts of Ireland round,
It would go hard to you to find
Anything else so beautiful anywhere;
And often I am lonely,
Looking at the Island and the gannets falling
And to hear the sea-tide lonely in the caves.
But sure 'tis an odd heart that is never lonely.'

TOMAS

THE day after my arrival on the Island, Tomás has been fishing all the morning over by Beiginis, and comes into the kitchen early in the afternoon carrying a large bream.

'That's a fine fish you have,' I say.

'It is for you, for I thought on the first day of your coming back to the Island you should have a good fish for supper.'

I take the fish and lay it down on the table, and begin to thank him in my halting Irish.

'Don't thank me till you have heard all my story,' says he.

'Well,' I say, 'no story could make any difference to my thanks.'

'Listen then. When I came back from fishing this morning I had two bream, one larger and one smaller. That one there is not the larger of the two.'

'How comes that?' I say, smelling a jest in the wind.

'Well, it was this way. I came into my house, and I laid the two fish down on the table, and I said to myself: "Now which of these two fish shall I give the gentleman from London?" And there came into my head the old saying, "When the Lord God made Heaven and earth at the first, He kept the better of the two for himself." And where could I find a higher example?'

Laughing together over this artfully prepared comedy, we go into the room at right angles to the kitchen which shelters the King's guests. We sit down at the table in front of the window, through which the eye ranges over the strait to the naked line of the coast of Ireland, and the business of the afternoon begins.

We have to discuss what form my lessons are to take.

I want to practise myself in writing down the language from his lips. What is he to give me, isolated words and sentences, or tales and poems? The verdict falls for the tales and, since the Island once possessed a poet, Seán Ó Duínnlé, for his poems set in the circumstances which provoked them. For in his life Tomás has seen and remembered many things, and he grew up to manhood, he tells me, in a livelier world.

'When I was a young man growing up,' he says, 'it was a different world from the world we have to-day. There was no silent drinking then, into the tavern and out of it without a word said, but you would be walking the road and the tavern-door would be open and you would go in. There would be as many as twenty men in the room drinking, and every man that came in he would not go out without singing a song or telling a tale. And you would go down into the street, there would be noise coming out of another tavern, and it would be the same there, tales a-telling and songs a-singing and no man quiet. You would hear no word of English in Dingle that time, but Irish only spoken through all the streets and houses. The country was full to the lid of songs and stories, and you would not put a stir out of you from getting up in the morning to lying down at night but you would meet a poet, man or woman, making songs on all that would be happening. It is not now as it was then, but it is like a sea on ebb, and only pools here and there left among the rocks. And it is a good thought of us to put down the songs and stories before they are lost from the world for ever.'

And so, he sitting on one side of the table, rolling a savoury sprig of dillisk round and round in his mouth to lend a salt flavour to his speech, and I diligently writing on the other side, the picture of the Island's past grew from day to day under our hands. At times I would stop

him as an unfamiliar word or strange twist of phrase
struck across my ear, and he would courteously explain
it, giving parallels from the local speech or illustrating
with a little tale, budded off, as it were, from the larger
unit. Thus on one occasion the phrase, 'the treacherous
horse that brought destruction on Troy', came into a song.

'And what horse was that?' I said.

'It was the horse of wood,' he answered, 'that was made
to be given to the King that was over Troy. They took
it with them and brought it into the very middle of the
city, and it was lovely to look upon. It was in that city
Helen was, she that brought the world to death; every
man that used to come with a host seeking her, there
would go no man of them safe home without falling
because of Helen before the city of Troy. It was said that
the whole world would have fallen by reason of Helen
that time if it had not been for the thought this man had,
to give the horse of wood to the King. There was an
opening in it unknown to all, two men in it, and it full of
powder and shot. When the horse was in the midst of the
city, and every one of them weary from looking at it, a
night of the nights my pair opened the horse and out with
them. They brought with them their share of powder and
shot. They scattered it here and there through the city
in the deep night; they set fire to it and left not a living
soul in Troy that wasn't burnt that night.'

Another word in a tale once provoked my inquiry,
bolg an tsoláthair it was, the providing bag.

'I've heard of that bag,' I said, 'but I never rightly
understood what it was.'

'There's a tale to that,' said Tomás. 'Put down your
pencil and I'll tell it to you.'

'A good number of years ago a company set out from
the capital of Ireland. They had made an arrangement

to collect new poems and songs new-made throughout the land. They were a league with money put together and their intention was to start out through the country and give a reward to everyone who should come with three stanzas of a song put together by himself. There was one of them set up in County Kerry, a house like a college in the middle of the town, a great big round table on one leg, and a heap of papers and books in the middle of it, clerks sitting all round it, money scattered all over it, every kind in a box of wood, and the money was to be had by everyone who liked to draw upon it, at the rate of from half a crown to a crown for every three stanzas according to their character and value.

'There were a score of tenants in this town in Kerry that they stopped in, and taken all round they had the grass of twenty cows, each one of them, and the town was quite close to the Great Lake of Killarney. Now when the business of the board was settled and everything shipshape, they set the people thinking. At first it was the children of the poor folk from beyond the limits of the town that carried off the money. Then the children of the strong farmers of the town saw how things were going, that more was to be made by putting together song stanzas and poems than to be labouring on the land as they were doing; and, thinking so, these children of the strong farmers gave up working the land and fell to making songs and poems. It didn't take long for their land to run to waste as they let it go anyhow. They didn't care, for the man that got least would have half a crown, another would get ten shillings, while any of them that had a ready wit would lift a pound every afternoon.

'Now there was a gentleman living some way from this town, and, when he saw the passion driving the people of the town with the board in it, he saw at once that the town would soon go to ruin at this wild rate, and that the landlord wouldn't let them get much into arrear when they wouldn't be able to pay the rent, for the landlords were mighty hard on the people in those days. The gentleman was right enough in his conjecture, for the board and the town didn't last long, they went at it together so wildly. The old people said that, whatever trouble this board brought on the town, nobody believed that the board got anything out of it either for the people that set it up.

'Not long after this the trouble came on the town, and they couldn't pay rent or rate, and the landlord was particularly enraged, for he saw that it was through their own folly and carelessness in working the land that they couldn't pay rent or rate. And the first visit he made to them was to throw them out pell-mell, leaving not a living soul of those twenty tenants in possession. Not long after their eviction, the gentleman on the other side came to the landlord with a purse of gold to pay the rent and rate, and he soon became a rich man. The others wandered off through the countryside with their children, and they were no matter of pity, for their own fault had brought about their ruin.'

There is no need for me to say that this anticipation of the Gaelic League is entirely apocryphal, and that of all the boards that have ever benefited or afflicted Ireland none ever went by the name of the Board of Poetry. And I cannot help thinking that Tomás was a little hard upon the unfortunate farmers, who at least provide an instance unique in history or legend of a town ruined by poetry. Towns have been ruined by so many worse things.

I remember, as I listened to the tale, some wandering association dropped into my mind the story of a Greek town regenerated by poetry, which Laurence Sterne stole, by way of Burton of the *Anatomy*, from Lucian. Let us listen to it here, that poetry may be vindicated.

'————The town of Abdera, notwithstanding Democritus lived there, trying all the powers of irony and laughter to reclaim it, was the vilest and most profligate town in all Thrace. What for poisons, conspiracies and assassinations—libels, pasquinades and tumults, there was no going there by day—'twas worse by night.

'Now, when things were at the worst, it came to pass, that the Andromeda of Euripides being represented at Abdera, the whole orchestra was delighted with it: but of all the passages which delighted them, nothing operated more upon their imaginations, than the tender strokes of nature which the poet had wrought up in that pathetic speech of Perseus,

　　　O Cupid, prince of God and men, &c.

Every man almost spoke pure iambics the next day, and talk'd of nothing but Perseus his pathetic address—"O Cupid, prince of God and men"—in every street of Abdera, in every house—"O Cupid! Cupid!"—in every mouth, like the natural notes of some sweet melody which drops from it whether it will or no—nothing but "Cupid! Cupid! prince of God and men" —The fire caught—and the whole city, like the heart of one man, open'd itself to Love.

'No pharmacopolist could sell one grain of helebore—not a single armourer had a heart to forge one instrument of death— Friendship and Virtue met together, and kiss'd each other in the street—the golden age return'd, and hung over the town of Abdera—every Abderite took his oaten pipe, and every Abderitish woman left her purple web, and chastely sat her down and listen'd to the song—'

From Abdera to Killarney is a far cry, and to the one poetry brought love, to the other ruin; but the last event is alike to both, for you will hear but little natural song in Abdera or Killarney to-day, and perhaps in neither does poetry get much reward, whether of love or money.

A HILL-SIDE PARLIAMENT

ON a September day of veiled light and trembling heat
I was standing on the crazy wall at the side of the
King's house, looking out over the mile of water between
Beiginis and the Island. Beyond Beiginis the water rolled
oilily, now and again lifting its unbroken surface in a
long wave as the swell of some distant Atlantic storm
came silently up the sound.

Within Beiginis the water was broken here and there
by little islands, and rocks emergent or awash over which
the lazy sea tumbled in a flutter of foam. The mainland
trembled in a false distance of summer mist, the customary
sharp outline of its hills lost upon an uncertain sky. On
all that three miles of sea nothing moved, no faintest wind
wrinkled the steely surface; there was not a boat to be
seen inshore or out in the sound, for the expected mackerel
shoal had not yet come, and the lobsters, said a fisherman
at my feet, 'had a summer sickness' and lay languid in
their holes among the rocks. Only over the water at our
feet three or four gannets were floating idly, poised in the
height of air upon almost moveless wings and searching
the sea with outstretched necks and unrelenting eyes.
From time to time one of the birds would descry or
imagine something in the water and, turning over in the
air, plunge sullenly down and disappear under the surface.
We could see the spurt of the water, and hear the splash
of that heavy body; and then, after an incredibly long
interval, up he would come with nothing in his beak, float
a moment on the water, lift himself with a visible effort,
circle round for a few minutes, and then, mounting the
air, rejoin his fellows in their everlasting, hopeless quest.
This plunge of the gannet the islanders call *buala*, 'striking',
and it is their test of the presence of fish. If the shoal had

come the air would be full of the great birds, floating and
falling, floating and falling the whole day through. But
now it was clear there were few fish in the sea. 'Níl an
t-iasg ann, mar dá mbeadh sé ann, bheadh an buachail
sin ag buala go tiubh', said my companion. 'There is no
fish there, for if there were that lad would be striking
thick and fast.'

I lost patience at last, overcome by the languor of the
day, and, leaping down from the wall, turned towards
the hill. Here, on the rough road that climbs the shoulder
of the land to the left, there was a semblance of activity.
A line of asses was strung out along its rising length, each
followed by a man or a child, the whole procession moving
upwards with a deliberate and painful slowness. Sometimes with an almost ritual gesture a man would bring his
hand down on the buttock of his ass, not with any Utopian
notion of accelerating its speed, for the Island asses run
only on one gear, but in a kind of friendly formality well
understood on both sides. Gradually the frieze of men and
beasts faded out over the hill shoulder. 'I'll go help carry
the turf,' said I. 'It's little help you'll bring, maybe,' said
the pessimist at my side, 'but go. It's a sultry day, and
there'll be great talking back on the hill.' Without another
word said, I turned and followed lazily up the road.

This road was made by the islanders themselves, under
the direction of a ganger from the Congested Districts
Board, in the year 1910. I have good reason to remember
the date, for it was my first year on the Island, and I too
worked on the road, wielding an inexpert pick amid the
mockery of the others, and taking long intervals of rest to
nurse my aching arms.

The road sidles up the hill above the houses, and
turning the shoulder runs straight along for a mile or so,
suspended between the steep mountain slope and the
falling cliffs. As you go, the whole immense panorama of

Dingle Bay unfolds beneath you, the long lines of the hills gradually closing in upon that vast field of moving water. On that September day, as we went west along the road, the morning mists slowly withered in the air, and the sun came out in an almost intolerable brightness, bringing colour and distinctness into the grey and quivering mono-tone of the early morning. The lines of the hills sharpened against the blue sky, and the long moving body of the water swam and glittered and varied through a thousand hues, as the white clouds drifted across it and little local winds hastened over the ripples and died away. Below us the tide ran upon the rocks with a relentless muttering, but from the whole expanse of the bay there came an indescri-bable sound, like an easy and prolonged breathing, a gigan-tic but far-away and muffled sigh, the very voice of silence heard in the sensitive recesses of the mind beyond the ear.

On such a day, but earlier in the year, I sat once by a turf-rick on the hill-side while Tomás fitted the sods into their place with careful and experienced hands. He would stop occasionally and lean over me, filling and lighting his pipe. We spoke of the loveliness of the day and the scene, and he broke out suddenly: 'If you were to walk all Ireland round it would come hard to you to find another place so beautiful as this. You can see the Skellig rocks and Valencia Island, the hills of Ibh Ráthach, and Dingle Bay, and Slea Head that lies farthest west into the sea of all Ireland. And away behind is Brandon Mountain, and round the corner is Cruach Mhárthain, that has for another name the Bed of Diarmaid and Gráinne. But Diarmaid never came there with Gráinne, but that was the station where he kept watch for Fionn, for there was a man of the Fian watching over every bay and harbour town in Ireland. And round there is Ventry, where the Fian fought for a year and a day with Dáire Donn, King of the world, and all the hosts of the world. You would be sitting here on a day of sun, and the water moving on the rocks and the trawlers from Dingle sailing the bay, and you would say to yourself that there was no place more beautiful in the world, east and west. And I do not say that it would not be true for you.'

I had caught up with the company now, and we moved along slowly, losing one of our number every now and then as a man and an ass detached themselves, to climb the slope where their own rick showed upon the side of the hill. When we had gone some way back along the Island we came upon a little group of men, the King one of them, lying on the grass sunning themselves and smoking, while their asses strayed and grazed about them. 'It's a parliament,' said one of the men with me, 'and the King on his throne in the middle of them.' I sat down among the rest, and the flood of talk, interrupted a moment by my coming, resumed its headlong flow. They had been discussing something I had said the night before about the earlier inhabitants of the Island. One of them turned to me, a little man whose face carries on it always an expression equally divided between a country shrewdness and an intense and puzzled surprise.

'They tell me, Bláheen,' he said (for that is the name I have on the Island, a diminutive for the Irish word for 'flower'), 'that you said last night that there were men living on the Island a thousand years ago.'

'There were,' I answered, 'and it's a wonder to me how they lived.'

'And who would they be? I've heard tell that the Danes were in it once.'

'Yes,' I said, 'the Danes were here once, but these were earlier than the Danes, men of religion.'

'By my baptism,' broke in another, a lean man with a wandering eye, 'you have the right of it. It's well I know how they came here at the first.'

'And how was that?'

'It was this way. There was a bloody queen of the English, the daughter of a king and a whore, and she renounced the Mass, and was hunting the priests everywhere and taking the heads off them every day. And it was so that some of the priests fled before her and came to this Island and hid themselves here from the pursuit, for they didn't want the heads taken off them, and small blame to them. Eilís was her name, and she was an evil woman.'

'No, it isn't like that the tale was,' I said. 'It's true that Queen Elizabeth hunted the priests, but it was a great while before her day that the men of religion lived here on the Island. You know the ruins at the back of the Island?'

'Indeed I do, the bright stone houses (*na clocháin gheala*) we call them. Did they live in those?'

'They did. And there are houses like them in other parts of Ireland, and the men of learning have it made out that they were built more than a thousand years ago, centuries before Queen Elizabeth came into the world.'

'I don't give in to that,' he cried out, with the ferocity of a man who, having once advanced a theory, is bound to defend it to the world's end.

'And why wouldn't you?' broke in another, 'when it's Bláheen that says it, one that has read all the books in the world?'

'Well,' said the sceptic, 'it may be that he has his belly full of books, but it isn't everything that is written in a book, and, what's more, there are a lot of lies to be found in those same books.'

At this the King took his pipe out of his mouth, spat with severity, and spoke.

'Now, aren't you the obstinate man!' he said. 'For it isn't only Bláheen that says it, but every scholar and man of learning that comes to the Island they are in the one tale of it. And it is my opinion that they are right. They were great workers of stone in the old times. Doesn't the proverb say that all things in the world are growing better but only poetry and the craft of stoneworking? And the men that put those houses together without mortar or lime, they had the craft of stoneworking if ever any man had.'

This settled the matter, for a proverb is a final argument not to be controverted.

'And have you any story of the Danes?'

'I have,' I answered, 'and, more than that, the Island has its name out of their language.'

'How do you make that out? Isn't its name An Blascaod Mór and isn't that Irish?'

'That is the name it has now and for a long while, but it had another name in the old times.'

'And how do you know that?'

'Well, I found it this way. Long ago, before there were maps or charts of the kind we have now, there were men in Italy that made charts of the coasts of the world, so that their ships could sail safely by them; and they wrote down the names of the towns and islands along the coasts. And in the earliest of these charts the name of this island is written Brasker, and that is the name for a sharp reef of rock in the language the old Danes spoke.'

'It was a great invention to find that out. I remember that the Norwegian that was here once—Marstrander was his name and a fine man he was—I remember that he found a stone and writing on it of the kind they had in the old times, and he said that it was his own people that had written it. And he used to say that it was a great pity that his people did not stay in the mastery of Ireland, for if they had the English would never have come into it.'

'Well, that is as it may be,' I said. 'The world puts

many changes from it, and one people comes up and another goes down. I have heard of that stone and seen a picture of it. Some say that it is in the old secret writing, and others say not, but there is no deciding now, for the stone is lost long since. Be that as it may, the men of the North were here and on the mainland too, for there are names of places—Smerwick, Baile na nGall and Gallarus—called by them or from them. And more, it is said that one of their great chiefs was baptized in the Catholic faith over on the Skelligs there.'

'That is a great wonder. But tell me, if the Danes were here once, how did they go out? For it is certain that there are none here now and for a great while past.'

'Nobody knows rightly how they went, but there is a tale about it that Tomás told me.'

'Sure, Tomás has a head full of tales, and every one more wonderful than the last. How does he tell it?'

'Have you ever heard of the heather ale?'

'I have surely.'

'Well, you know then that that was the ale the Danes made out of the heather and a root that grows among the heather. And the root has this property, that, if the cattle eat of it they grow fat, and it puts a gloss upon their coats. And on the ale made out of the tops of the heather and this root a man can live with that only for his food.'

'It's little wonder they lived easily if they wanted only that for food.'

'Now in the end the Danes were all killed but two men only, a father and a son, and the secret of the heather ale was handed down from father to son, and at the last it had come to these two, and no other living man knew it. So the others brought these two to the top of the highest cliff in the Island, and asked them would they tell them the secret of the heather ale, or, if they wouldn't, down with them into the sea. Well, the father took the leader of the others on a sod apart, and said, if he would throw his son down, he would tell them the secret, for he had shame to tell it before the boy. So they took the boy and threw him down. And then the father said: "Throw me down too, for you shall never know the secret of the heather ale." And they threw him down.'

The general gasp of appreciation which greeted the dramatic conclusion of this tale was broken by a sad voice saying: 'It was a great sin of them to take away the secret of so good a drink. For what good could it do them and they dead?'

A moment later, as though at a signal, all the speakers in this 'parle on a hill' rose up, and the King said meditatively: 'Well, talking never brought the turf home yet'; and, each recovering his ass, they scattered slowly over the wide sweep of the rick-dotted hill.

At last I was left alone, sitting with my back against a rock, my hands clasped about my knees; and, looking out over the bay where the trawlers from Dingle were at work, I thought how faint and fallacious a memory the generations of men leave behind them, hardly more substantial than those flaws and eddies of wind that wrinkled for a moment the unchanging surface of the water, and died away into the vast indifference of the general sea.

Solitude

THEY could not stack the turf in that wet spring,
And the cold nights were icy in our bones,
And so we burned furze and the rusted bracken.
I climbed the hill alone
And by the old fort gathered in the sun
Red fern and crackling furze;
And, as I worked, a mist came from the sea
And took the world away,
And left me islanded in that high air,
Where the trenched doon broods silent on the hill.
I do not know what shapes were in the mist,
But solitude was made more solitary
By some re-risen memory of the earth
That gathered round my loneliness,
And threatened with the dead my living breath.
I could have cried aloud for a sharp fear,
But the mist thinned and withered, and the sun
At one swift stride came through.
They passed, those shadowy threats,
And the great company of Ireland's hills,
Brandon and Slemish and the lesser brethren,
Stood up in the bright air,
And on the other side the sea,
The illimitable Atlantic, rolled and shone.

Brendan

SOMETIMES I dream the whole rock-girdled island,
Adorned with the pale grasses and high ferns
And delicate faint-hued blossoms of the cliffs,
Floats insubstantial on the sea
Like the upthrust back
Of the huge fish Iasconius, where much-wandering
And far-adventuring Brendan held the Easters
Year after year of that long pilgrimage.
For this is Brendan's sea,
And yonder Brendan's mountain cloud-encompassed
Stands lonely in the sky;
And here he pondered over the strange splendour
That led him on, island to island, lost
In the vague, unpathed, unvoyageable sea,
Till in the twilight of the polar ocean
Huge ice-hills, ghostly in the ghostly sky,
Loomed over his frail boat,
And on one gleaming pinnacle there clung
A chained and brooding shape,
Iscariot, caught one day's length out of Hell.

THE BRIGHT DWELLINGS

I SET my face to the hill again, and now took my way against the slope, ascending slowly to the summit of the Island. There, almost on the highest ridge, where the land breaks abruptly towards the sea, an ancient people in days before any history had built their high place. Using the cliff-edge for the seaward front of their dún, they had drawn a semicircular trench to fence off their dwelling towards the land. And through a gap in the inner wall of this trench they had run a lesser ditch, dividing the inner space into two equal portions. The whole forms a cliff fort of the kind familiar along the range of the sea-wall of southern and western Ireland.

Let us leave it to the historians of the time before history to inquire who were the dark and strange people before the coming of the Celts who, vanishing, have left little more than these vast shells in which they lived to be their memorials. We cannot penetrate to the thoughts that thrilled them as they looked out over the cliff-wall across the shoreless sea towards the sunset. It may be that, when we stand in their place and, forgetting all the memories of our young civilizations, abandon ourselves to the unguided wantonness of feeling, some shadow of the thoughts that moved them drifts across our minds, out of reach of our treacherous apprehension, and they live again for the moment in the latest of their successors. Standing there, as the sea-mists crept over the Island and shut out the visible world, I have at times lost consciousness of this present earth and felt the illusion of other presences in the wreathing swirls of cloud; my mind has filled with fragile thoughts insubstantial as the mist itself, and known the terror of that loneliness in which the greatest fear is that we are not all alone. But the frail mists fade rapidly into the sun, and the light of the living will frightens back into the depths of the mind those ghostly memories older than ourselves that live below the surface of our thoughts.

The dún has known other inhabitants than those its first builders. Roughly shaped stones hidden in the earth bear witness to later buildings, and these may well have been the homes of men of religion whose constructions still remain elsewhere on the Island and in the other islands of the group. There may be some truth, too, in the tradition of the islanders which claims so confidently that the Danes dwelt here. That the Northmen were on the Island we may be confident, and they can hardly have failed to make use of this strong place commanding both the landward and the seaward slopes. But history has nothing to tell us of that occupation, and no monuments remain to fill the gap of the written record.

Below the fort the sharp wall of the cliff drops to a flat space, overgrown with heath, and fern, and sea-pink, and I know not what of the delicate and faint-hued island flowers. This space the islanders with a happy instinct call the garden of the dún. A path leading out of it to the left wanders down the cliff, and, if you have the head for heights, you may follow it and come at last to a hole under a flat ledge of rock called Sgairt Phiarais, Pierce's Cave, where, says the tradition, Pierce Ferriter, poet and warrior, hid from his enemies. Of Pierce's sojourn in the cave, and the poem he made there, we shall speak again.

Another path leads along the brink of the cliffs and climbs to the summit of An Cró, the highest point of the Island. Beneath to the sea are the 'bright stone dwellings' (*na clochán gheala*) of that conversation on the hill. Loose stones lie about all over the ground, and it is plain that there must at one time have been a considerable settlement here. It may be that excavation would reveal the foundations of a

church, but a cursory inspection does not yield any
evidence of such a building to the inexperienced eye.
Farther down towards the sea there is a little group of
ruins the form of which is still discernible. These have
been beehive huts of the customary Irish type. Of one
there are still considerable remains, of a very interesting
form. The building is half buried in the earth, and when
you come to examine it you find that it was originally
two-roomed, the rooms divided off from each other by an
interior wall with a low doorway. Other remains in the
neighbourhood are too fragmentary for description.

No record or tradition remains to tell what manner of
men dwelt here when these buildings were new. But other
such clocháns are to be found on Inis Tuaisceart and
Inisicíleáin, and there can be little doubt that they had
an ecclesiastical purpose. This is the country of St.
Brendan. There across the water is the great mountain
named after him, where the country people go on painful
pilgrimage for the cure of all their ailments. And away
beyond Sybil Head is the bay from which in their tradition
he set out on his wild journey into the Atlantic, voyaging
among marvellous islands, and coming at last to that icy
peak where Judas Iscariot once in every year finds a day's
solace from the pains of Hell.

There is another story, found in a fifteenth-century
manuscript, that a pilgrim from these parts in the old
time went to Rome and remained there, marrying a
daughter of Rome, and begetting a son who afterwards
came to be the great Pope Gregory, Gregory of the Gael,
Gregory Goldenmouth. The natives of the papal city,
we know, have a different opinion in this matter, but
that, no doubt, is a mere local partiality. In any case,
when Pope Gregory was near his end, he gave instructions
that, when the breath had left his body the empty corpse
should be enclosed in a coffin with his name legibly

inscribed thereon, and that the coffin should be committed to the Tiber. So it was done, and Tiber carried the rich freight to the Mediterranean Sea, the current swept it through the Pillars of Hercules, and after long travel it was cast up on the shores of Aran; and there the golden-mouthed Pope found burial, an Irishman in Irish earth. In witness of which fact one of the sounds of Aran has the name of Gregory Sound to this day.

Everywhere on the shores of Dingle Bay are sacred spots: the oratory of Gallarus, a marvel of building, still whole and unimpaired, the church of Kilmalcadar, and the holy pyramid of Skellig Michael. One suspects some connexion between the ruins on the Blasket and the more perfect remains on the Great Skellig, which a local tradition says were a penitential settlement from a monastery on the mainland dedicated to St. Michael. It may be so, but one thinks rather of the other high places under the invocation of St. Michael of Monte Gargano, St. Michael in peril of the sea on the Breton coast, and the mount of St. Michael in Cornwall. Here, in these rocky fastnesses devoted to the warrior angel, the hermits may well have thought that their long battle against the demon hosts might best be carried to a conclusion. Cut off from all the easy ways of the world, with all the issues of life simplified in that savage isolation to an unrelenting conflict of prayer and fasting, they offered themselves up for their fellows in a white martyrdom of utter privation.

It is difficult for us, in a world which has followed other ways, to reach back again through so many centuries to those passionate and unreasoned simplicities. But here, in the arena of their conflict, standing in those humble huts of rough stone, we can put a hand on the broken wall, and through that contact something of that dedication of the eager heart is in part revealed to us. These

men had no need to go out into the world to find their
adversaries. The whole air up to Heaven was filled for
them with the black host of Satan, besieging every moment
of their day, waking, sleeping, standing, sitting, walking,
resting; hidden behind every thought, creeping in through
all the avenues of sense.

So beset, their chief wall of defence was the constant and
attentive recitation of the Psalter, the battle-songs of the
universal church. And to this sure shield they added
their own prayers and litanies, which bear upon them the
marks of this urgent warfare. These litanies, that have
no congregational character, are the most characteristic
remains of the old Irish Church. We cannot doubt that,
if indeed these ruins were the homes of Irish monks, they
must have heard passionate voices repeating again and
again, in the agony of spiritual battle, prayers and suppli-
cations differing hardly at all from those which have come
down to us on the time-stained vellum of our manuscripts.
And I like to think that the prayer of Maelísa Ó Brolcháin,
in which he invokes St. Michael to be with him in life and
death, represents in a later age the cry which went up
from these rocks when the bright stone dwellings were new,
and the hermit monks, in peril of the sea and of devils,
called on the armed archangel for present help in their
time of trouble.

> Hither flying,
> Michael of the miracles,
> Bear to God my crying.
>
> Dost thou hear?
> Seek of gracious God forgiveness
> Of my sinning vast and drear.
>
> Make no stay,
> Carry all my love and longing
> To the God of Gods away.

Swiftly bring
To my soul thy help and housel
When from prison it takes wing.

Come with might
To the soul that waits and wonders,
All the angel hosts in flight!

Wårrior saint,
'Gainst the whole world's crooked cunning
Give me courage when I faint.

In good will
Scorn not thou my painful praying,
While I live be with me still.

Thee I crave;
Free at last my sinful spirit,
Mind and heart and body save.

My pleader be,
When in that last battle breaking
Antichrist is slain by thee.

THE VILLAGE

L OOKING at the Great Blasket from the sea below, or from the hill above, you see the whole human settlement on the Island plainly, as on a relief map. But in the few years that I have known the Island the aspect of that settlement has changed greatly—more, probably, than in all the previous years of its existence. For I came first in the first year of that change. After many strange adventures with landlords and their agents—the landlords were sometimes decent men, they will tell you, but the agents were devils one and all—the Island had been taken over by the Congested Districts·Board, and was undergoing the process known to all the West as 'striping'. The old medieval common-field system, under which one man owned strips of land scattered over the whole area, in a fashion only identifiable by an expert in traditional lore, was giving way in a moment to the system under which each family has its land concentrated in convenient blocks of arable and pasture. You may imagine the process of ingenious and complicated judging by which this metamorphosis was effected.

It is one of the great regrets of my life that this happened at a time when my knowledge of Irish was so rudimentary that I could not follow the arguments that went on round me, turning the conversational surface of the Island, if I may be allowed the term, into the semblance of a sea in storm. I could see and hear the waves running high and throwing off their foaming crests of rhetoric under the winds of passion, but I understood as little of the purport of the tumult as one does of the rumour of raging waters. Every man had a nice appreciation of the qualities and tricks of his scattered strips, how they acted in all weathers, the run of the water through them, how potatoes came best in this place and oats in that—a whole complex system of traditional knowledge handed down from father to son, by which alone, it seemed, the niggard, unkindly earth could be persuaded to yield them sustenance. All this was now to go, and none would be satisfied unless the new unified allotments combined in a like proportion all the various properties of those scattered strips.

The work was already proceeding when I came, and I only descried as in a glass darkly the features of that change. It was long before the noise of the debate died down, but now I think the old system is almost forgotten, and the conveniences of the new have silenced the echoes of that storm. For the concentrated fields are easier to work, and the improved fencing keeps the animals from the crops much more securely than in the old time. The asses roaming in the night will even now sometimes leap the new walls, braving the fangs of the barbed wire, and make a ruin of the crops of young oats. But in the old days the fields were far less defensible, even in cases where, as sometimes happened, a man had his property together defended by such fencing as they had in those times. Tomás has a curious tale of a colt which swam the mile of sea from Beiginis to the Great Island, and destroyed a field of oats before his invasion was discovered.

'In the old time', so the tale runs, 'there lived a small farmer in the Western Island. He had a fine field of oats growing, and it well fenced, the way he thought no four-footed animal would come near it. He had his way with things for a while, for everything that he had growing, both potatoes and oats, was in that same patch. When he had it all settled he was quite content. He did not go to see his crops at all for a good while, for he thought no creature would go over the dyke among them. But one

day he went to his field of oats. His eyes opened when he
saw it, for it was all upside-down, broken and beaten, and
the most of it devoured on him. He was not so pleased
coming home as he was when he went out, and he said
the devil might have him if he didn't make the creature
that had done it pay for it.

'That was all very well. He got himself ready for the
night with his good pike so that he could make a clean
sweep of whatever it was that had ruined his oats on him.
He spent a good share of the night watching, but he heard
nothing and he saw nothing. He had more than half the
night spent that way in the end till he said to himself that
it wouldn't come to-night whatever thing it was. Off
home he went in the middle of the night, and he went to
bed, and he wasn't long gone when the horse came into
the oats after him and ate a good fill of them. When he
went to the oats in the morning after sleeping his enough,
he saw the fresh trail through them. He almost went out
of his wits, to see his fine field of oats ruined and no good
in them for ever, and another thing, him with no jot of an
idea what had done it.

'In the next night he swore the same oath that he would
go watching the oats to-night as well, and he wouldn't
leave till the day would lighten from the east on him on
the morrow. So it was. Away with him for the night, and
he stretched himself out by the dyke and waited there,
meaning not to slumber or sleep until the day on the
morrow. When he had more than half the night spent, a
glance that he gave across the field what should he see but
my lump of a horse dragging at the sprouting crop, long,
strong, and fierce. He made one leap only with the pike
in his hand to give it a jab. He couldn't reach it, and
instead of the horse turning towards the hill from him, it
was for the sea it made. There was a white sandbeach
under the field, and the horse made no stay till it reached

the strand, and the man thought that it meant to have a race on the sand after filling its belly. He followed it down to the strand, and he wasn't long till he saw the horse going down into the water and breasting the sea. The man blackened and reddened with rage to think that he had found out the horse, that his oats were ruined on him, and he going home with no satisfaction for it all.

'When he got home, his wife and children asked him did he see anything the length of the night. He said he had seen a lump of a horse in the oats, and when he put it out it set its face to the white strand. "Is he on the strand still?" said his wife. "He is not," says he. "Where did he go from you?" said she. "In the divil's name," says he, "he went out into the sea from me, and," says he, "the only fear I have is that he will come to the house to me when he has the oats eaten, and it isn't long he'll be over that." "What sort of colour was he?" says the wife. "I thought he was black," says he, "but he had a white patch on his forehead." "By this book!" says the eldest son, "there's his like of a horse grazing in Beiginis, and as I live," says he, "it's the same swims over every night to eat your share of oats; and I'll bet you," says he, "if you go into the strand to-morrow and look close at the foot of the track, you'll see more than one hoof-print." It was true for him. When the day came his father went down to the strand, and when he looked at the foot of the track he found a score or so hoofmarks there. He recognized then that it was one of the horses that were at grass, and indeed it was. The colt belonged to a man from Ventry parish. The farmer warned him about the horse when he recognized it, and he had to come and take it out of Beiginis, though it hadn't half the grass eaten, and he had to pay for the whole season's grass. But that didn't leave any oats for the island farmer, for he hadn't a single sheaf that year through the horse.'

This change in the agricultural system was accompanied by another change which has even more profoundly affected the aspect of the Island from the sea. Many of the houses, crouching low in the hollows of the hill-slope, had gone rotten with time and exposure, and seemed as I remember them hardly fit for human habitation. And so the Board condemned the worst of them, and planned the building of new houses out in the space between the hill and the crops. These houses stand in a sharp contrast to the older type. The old houses huddle together on the broken hill-slope above the cliffs, thrown down without system wherever a convenient site has offered itself, and steep little tracks run hither and thither between them. They are cabins of the ordinary Irish style, a great rectangular shell built of roughly shaped stones mortared with mud, and washed with white or yellow lime over more or less of the exposed surface. They are roofed now with timber covered with tarred felt, but this is not the ancient fashion. In the memory of the old men they were thatched with rushes, which rotted easily in the rains and let through the constant drip—*an braon anuas*—of which so much is said in proverbs and traditional poems. The hens would flutter up on to the thatch, attracted by the crawling life that swarmed there, and it was their custom to make holes in the thatch and lay their eggs there. The old men remember how as children they would clamber up and search the holes in the roof, coming down triumphantly to their mothers with a clutch of eggs from the carefully hidden nests. It would be a sanguine hen that should attempt to lay an egg upon the black and slippery felt to-day. The only decoration of the roofs now are the shapeless slabs of salt fish—pollock and bream and conger—which lie there curing in the sun, turning gradually to a dirty, unpalatable white.

Within, the rafters are exposed, and at each end an

open loft runs out into the room just below the spring of
the roof. The loft at the bottom of the house is *an lochta*—
the loft proper—while the *cúllochta*, the back-loft, over-
hangs the hearth. Beneath this back-loft is the stone
hearth, with its fire of turf, and, in the older houses, a
great open chimney down which the light of day shines
dimly through the smoke. Beside the hearth stands a
gallows-shaped erection with a swinging arm, from which
depends the graduated rack suspending over the fire at
varying heights the kettle and iron pots, the sole cooking
implements of the Island.

Under the loft at the lower end a room is boarded off,
an seomra, the chamber, the room *par excellence*, the rest of
the house being always spoken of as the kitchen. The
room contains a bed, a chair or two, washing materials,
and a chest. The furniture of the kitchen is equally simple,
all for use, not luxury; a settle which can be used as a bed,
and has an infinite capacity as a seat in the daytime, a
table equally accommodating when there is a call for
seats, a dresser boarded in below to serve on occasion as a
hen-coop, and a few chairs either of wood or woven cords.
The walls are lime-washed, in some cases yellow, or yellow
with a broad pink border below, from the floor to about
half the height of a man, in others a peculiarly unhealthy
and gloomy shade of red.

The same wall decorations appear with a monotonous
regularity in all the houses. There are religious pictures
bought from travelling pedlars, a Virgin and Child, or a
Christ with sorrowing eyes and rent and flaming heart,
crowned with thorns, the emblem of the devotion of the
Sacred Heart, before which a tiny brass lamp burns always
with a thin flame showing through red glass. These are
executed in a style of trade realism, smoothly and oilily
naturalistic. But one picture which now appears in most
of the houses is of a different and nobler tradition. During

the troubles a Dublin publisher had the happy inspiration to produce a print of Nostra Domina de Succursu, Our Lady of Succour, modelled upon a Byzantine original, a Virgin and Child in bright colours on a gold ground with red Greek lettering, preserving in its last degradation the air of unearthly dignity which that rigid religious convention can never lose. You might go far before you found a better example of the advantage of a formal over a realistic tradition. The contrast shows with an even sharper emphasis in the trade almanacs which American relations from Springfield or Holyoke send home to their families on the Island, adorned with girls of an inane prettiness leaning over rustic gates or riding on high-stepping horses groomed to an incredible shininess.

The loft over the fire is heaped with implements of the Island existence: nets, bags of wool, sails, oars, ladders, boots, and concertinas, shears for sheepshearing and panniers for turf-carrying, an epitome and index of all that simple life. Some of these overflow into the other loft, but that is commonly used for a supplemental bedroom, and is sometimes boarded in and lit by a window in the lower gable.

Such, more or less, is the aspect and the furniture of the older houses. The newer houses, built by the Board, are at once contrasted with, and assimilated to, the old fashion. The first thing that strikes one about them is their utter lack of adaptation to the Island conditions. The older houses, as we have seen, cuddle down into the earth out of the wind and weather, but these stand gauntly up out of the bare hill-side, and the wind and the rain and the flying surf of winter beat relentlessly upon the whole of their surface. They are strongly built of cement, and in place of the lofts have an upper story under their slate roofs. This upper story was a mystery to some of their future inhabitants when they were first designed. I remember well how one of the men, though he must often have seen houses of a similar make in Dingle, could not at first be brought to understand what an upper story meant. The site of his new house had been marked out on the hill-side, and he would often be seen, a forlorn figure in the evening light, pacing the bare turf within the marks of the ground-plan, and muttering to himself that he was being cheated, for the space was less than the area of his own house, and he could not get it into his head that the upstairs rooms would more than double his accommodation. With the little Irish I had then I made desperate attempts to explain the mystery, but he was never completely at ease until the walls had risen and he could see for himself how great a gain was his.

These five new houses stand in an irregular line a little way up from the road which runs above the cultivated ground, and at night their lighted windows can be seen from the opposite mainland. Their naked commonplaceness is one of the first impressions you have as you approach the Island across the Sound. But, if you open one of the doors and go in, you will find that the kitchen has been entirely assimilated to the general type. Two things are different. The floor is of cement in place of the earth and boards of the older houses. And opposite the door a wooden stair with a rail runs up into the bedrooms. This is a great addition to the seating resources of the house, and on a night of assembly, a dance, or other occasion, an ascending line of boys and girls sits from stair to stair, till at last the final couple are visible only as four legs showing below the level of the ceiling.

For the rest, the furniture, the pictures, the whole economy and arrangement of the room, are exactly as in the older houses, and only the roaring of the wind over the roof in days of storm reminds you that you are living under a new dispensation. And since the houses are so high up among the gusts, the fire is more sensitive of the direction of the wind, and when it blows from certain points of the compass the room fills with smoke, which catches you by the throat and brings on a smarting in the eyes. In other respects the houses seem much more convenient, and make up in comfort the wrong they do to the picturesque aspect of the Island. But with their coming something of the old world passed away, for the older type of house was in a right harmony with its surroundings, while these high and bare constructions stand in a perpetual contradiction of the whole environment of hill and sea and sky in which they are so violently set down.

The Dance

ON the white wall flickered the sputtering lamp
And lit the shadowy kitchen, the sanded floor,
The girls by the painted dresser, the dripping men
Late from the sea and huddled,
These on the settle, those by the table; the turf
Sent up faint smoke, and faint in the chimney a light
From the frost-fed stars trembled and died,
Trembled and died and trembled again in the smoke.
'Rise up now, Shane', said a voice, and another:
'Kate, stand out on the floor'; the girls to the men
Cried challenge on challenge; a lilt in the corner rose
And climbed and wavered and fell, and springing again
Called to the heavy feet of the men; the girls wild-eyed,
Their bare feet beating the measure, their loose hair flying,
Danced to the shuttle of lilted music weaving
Into a measure the light and the heavy foot.

PEIG

ONE autumn day I strolled along the road, which was full of men and women, girls and boys coming home from the fields, each one a moving stack of oatsheaves, for they were bringing in the harvest. I myself had helped in that work the day before, and was paying for it now by an intolerable pain in the back and loins where I had almost broken in two under the burden of the sheaves.

I turned now out of the road and approached one of the new houses. The door was open as I came to it, and I heard a clear, firm, woman's voice lifted in anger. I stepped over the threshold and was greeted in this fashion:

'The devil eat you between earth and sky! Get out!'

I stood still in surprise, and was almost knocked over by an ass hastily decamping, with the owner of the voice following at his tail.

'God with us! is it you, Bláheen?' she said.

'It is,' said I, 'but what have I done that you give me to the devil to eat between earth and sky?'

'Ah! You know well it wasn't you I was cursing, but the ass, for he's the thief of the world, and my heart's broken driving him out of the house. But come in and welcome; for you know well that it isn't curses but blessings that you'll always find before you in this house. And sit up to the fire on the chair and take your ease. It was only this morning I was wondering what had come to you, for you haven't crossed my threshold for three days.'

I walked up the floor to the fire and sat down, leaning over and spreading my hands to the smouldering turf, as one does automatically, even on a warm autumn day like this. She sat on a low stool on the other side of the hearth, and, taking a pipe from the hole in the wall at the back of the fire, picked up a burning fragment of turf in the tongs, set it on the bowl of the pipe, and began to draw the smoke through the short stem.

'The people of the Island have a fine gift of cursing,' I said.

'We have,' she answered, 'but there is no sin in it. If the curses came from the heart, it would be a sin. But it is from the lips they come, and we use them only to give force to our speech, and they are a great relief of the heart.'

'Well,' I said, 'I make little of them, for if the blessings come from the heart I don't care where the curses come from.'

And we fell to discussing the powers of the Irish language, and the falling away in these days from the uses of the old times when the tellers of tales went from place to place, competing against one another, and each was at pains to make his speech apt and clever, and to put a gloss upon his tales so that he might have a victory over the others. For Big Peg—Peig Mhór—is one of the finest speakers on the Island; she has so clean and finished a style of speech that you can follow all the nicest articulations of the language on her lips without any effort; she is a natural orator, with so keen a sense of the turn of phrase and the lifting rhythm appropriate to Irish that her words could be written down as they leave her lips, and they would have the effect of literature with no savour of the artificiality of composition. She is wont to illustrate her talk with tales, long and short, which come in naturally along the flow of conversation, and lighten up all our discourse of the present with the wit and wisdom and folly and vivid incident of the past.

To-day our talk, after touching lightly on this and that, turned to dreams and their meaning, and in a little I found myself telling a story of a dream of my own.

'You have said, Peig,' I began, 'that dreams have a meaning, and that sometimes they come to pass after we have dreamt them.'

'Well,' she answered, 'some come to pass and some do not, but it is not easy to tell always which is which.'

'Then,' I said, 'tell me which of the two is a dream that I had in the spring of this year. For I dreamt I was sitting alone in my room in London, and there came a knock at the door. So I cried, "Come in," and a boy came in and said: "There is a gentleman to see you, sir." And I said: "What is his name?" "Mr. James Smith, sir." "Well, show Mr. James Smith in," I said. And Mr. James Smith came in. He was a little lean dark man, a man that didn't look too honest, and he had a battered round black hat in one hand, and in the other hand a ragged little black bag. So I said: "Well, Mr. Smith, can I do anything for you?" "Yes, Mr. Flower," he said, "with your leave I should like to show you a few photographs." "Well," I said, "if you think they would please me, show them to me." And he came up to where I was sitting, and began to pour photographs out of the little black bag on to the table in front of me. The photographs came out of the bag one after another, and a few of them were of people I knew, some of my friends, some of them the people whose pictures you see in the newspapers, but for the most part I knew none of them. This went on for a long time, and I began to wonder, for more photographs were coming out of the bag than so small a bag could hold. And I was just about to say that I could not understand why he was showing me these photographs, when a photograph of myself appeared on the table. I stopped him then, and, "Tell me, Mr. Smith," I said, "why have you put my photograph with all these others?" Then he began to stammer and go red, and "Oh, I beg your pardon, Mr. Flower," he said, "I ought not to have shown you the photographs like this, I should have told you what they are first." "What are they then?" I said. "They are the photographs of the people who are going to die this year," he said; and with that he vanished out of my sight as though the earth had swallowed him. And I promise you that I woke up sweating, and it was many days before I put the horror of that dream from me. Is that one of the dreams that come to pass? for, if it is, I have not long to live.'

'That's a strange tale,' said Peig. 'But it isn't a vision, only a dream. For there are three kinds of things that come to us when we are asleep: dreams, that are only strange stories that pass through the mind in sleep, nightmares, that are nothing but fears of the night, and visions, that are of things that come to pass. And yours was only a dream, and you will not die this year.'

I could not understand by what means Peig made the distinction, but she was right, and I did not die that year. She went on to say that not only did we see visions of things that were to come to pass in sleep, but there were such things as waking visions.

'There was a young man once living in Ventry parish,' she said, and I knew by the traditional opening that a tale was coming, 'and one day his people all went to Dingle, and he stayed alone at home in the farm. And, when he had done what he had to do about the farm, he came into the kitchen and sat down by the fire, and was looking at the smoke coming from the sods and thinking. But what he was thinking about I never heard, so I cannot tell you. And he wasn't long thus when the latch was lifted, and the door opened and an old woman came in. "God save you," said she. "Long life to you," said he, "and welcome." She sat down by the hearth, and, "Would you give me a glass of milk and a piece of bread?" said she, "for I am long walking the roads, and the day is hot and I am tired. And I am only a poor old tramping woman, and, if you give help to the likes of me, God will reward you with long life and Heaven at the end of it." "I will do that," said he. So he rose and brought her a glass of milk and a piece of bread; and more than that, when she had drunk the milk and eaten the bread, he gave her a piece of money.

' "You have been good to me," she said, "and since good ought to be requited with good, I will show you something." So she told him to get her a bowl of hot water, and he put the kettle on the fire, and when the water was hot he poured it into a bowl, and she put the bowl in the middle of the floor. Then she took something from her pocket, and she scattered it over the water in the bowl, and said some words over the bowl, but what the words were he could not make out. He was sitting all this time by the fire, saying nothing, but, when the steam rose from the bowl after she had said the words, the door opened and a young girl came in and walked up to the fire. She stood there gazing down into the fire, and he was looking at her, and he saw all her form and feature, but he did not know her, for he had never seen her before. And the steam passed from the bowl as the water cooled, and the girl turned down from the fire and walked out of the door, and he did not see her any more.

' So he turned to the old tramping woman and said to her: "Who was that girl?" "That is the girl that you will marry," she said, and she told him what age the girl was then, and at what time he should marry her; and then she asked the blessing of God on him for the kindness he had done her, and she went out of the door and he never saw her again. But in the time she had said he went to Dunquin parish one day, and he met a girl there, and it was the girl he had seen in the vision. And they fell in love with one another and were married. And do you know who that girl was?'

'How should I know?' I said, 'for I never heard the tale before, and I suppose the thing happened in the old times before you or I came into the world.'

'It happened before I came into the world anyhow,'

she said, 'for the young man was my father and the girl
was my mother, and it's often my father told me that
same story.'

'And I suppose it was not the only story he told you,
Peig?' I said.

'You may say that, for he was the best teller of a tale
that ever was in this country-side. Tomás Sayers was
his name.'

'Sayers?' I said. 'Why, that is an English name.'

'Yes, and it was from England his people came in the
old times. And they were Protestant by faith until my
grandfather's time, and then they turned to the Catholic
faith. My father had more tales than any man of his
time, and if you had heard him telling them you would
have wondered, for he never forgot anything but went
right on, one thing after another, all the tale as it happened
and all the sayings and ways of speech, he had them all
better than any other man. He lived to be ninety-six
years old, and till a day or two before his death he could
tell any tale without stopping or staying, and his mind
was as clear and his speech as good as it had ever been.
He was a little, lively man, and the boys of the village
used to come to our house over there in Dunquin at night
to hear him story-telling.

'He had a bed at the side of the kitchen, and one night
the boys had come in to the tale-telling, and they were
sitting round the fire, and one of them turned to my
father and said: "Abair sgéal a Thomáis," tell us a tale.
So he began on a tale, An Damh Dearg—"The Red
Ox"—it was, and everybody knows that that is a long and
complicated tale. But he went right on telling it till he
came to the middle of the tale. Then he stopped suddenly,
and his tongue was tied for a while, and he stumbled in
the tale. And never before had I known him at a loss in a
tale. But in a little while he came to himself again, and he

took up the tale and told it straight through to the end.
And when he had finished I rose and went over to him,
and said, "You stumbled in that tale, Father," I said.
"I did," he said. "Well," said I, "never before have I
known you to stumble in a tale. And that is a sign that
death is near to you." "Dhera," he said, "Death hasn't
left Cork on his way to me yet." Then we all went to bed,
and in the middle of the night he cried out, and I went to
him, and he was sitting up in bed with fear in his eyes, and
"He has struck me," he said, "I have his blow in my
heart"; and from that time he sickened and two days
later he was dead.'

'God rest his soul,' I said, 'that was a good end for a
teller of tales.'

'It was,' she said, and we turned back to discuss the
vision he had seen of the young girl that was to be his
wife.

'There are many tales of the ghosts of the dead,' I said,
'but that is the first tale I have heard of the ghost of a
living person.'

'Do you believe,' she asked, 'that there are ghosts,
spirits of people that have gone from this world, and come
back in the night to visit the living?''

'Well, I have heard many tales of them, but I have
never seen a ghost myself, and I do not know anybody
who has certain knowledge of them. But there are many
strange things in the world beyond our knowledge, and
maybe there are ghosts too, though I do not understand
why they should come back to this world when they have
gone from it. It would be better for them to rest in their
graves and not be bothering us.'

'I have not seen a ghost either,' she said, 'but I have
known people who have, and there are many tales of
them, and of strange things that happen upside down
with the things of this world. There was a lad in Ventry

parish once, and he could not make a living in the place where he was, so he said to himself that he would travel to the north of Ireland, and that maybe he would find something to do there that would bring a bite of food to his mouth. And he set out with a friend from the same parish, and they walked Ireland till they came to the north, and there they took service with a farmer, and were doing well for a time. But after a time this lad fell sick, and he called his friend to him, and said, "I know that I am going to die." "Don't say that," said his friend. "I do say that, for, young or old, when the day comes, we must go. But I always thought, when I came to die, to be buried in my own churchyard among my kindred, and now I am dying a long way from home. But promise me this much, that when I am dead you will cut the head off me, and take that and bury it in my own churchyard.' His friend was unwilling at first, but at the last he gave the promise, and the lad died happy, for he knew that some part of him would rest in his own churchyard.

'So, when he died, his friend was true to his word, and he cut the head from him and started throughout Ireland with the head wrapped in a cloth. And at last he came to Ventry parish, weary with walking, and he turned into the house of his friend, and he put the cloth with the head in it on the table, and told them that it was their son's head, that he had died in the north, and that he had wished that his head should be buried in his own churchyard, since his body could not rest there. And they got in a coffin, and a barrel of porter and some tobacco pipes, and had a wake on the head. And the next day they started for Ventry churchyard with the head in the coffin. You know that Ventry churchyard is in a place where two roads meet. Now, as they came down their road they saw another funeral coming down the other road. Now it is the custom, when two funerals are coming to the same churchyard at the same time, for them to race together so that the one that wins will be the first to bury its dead. So they made all speed down their road, and the other funeral hastened down the other road. And they came together in the same moment to the wall of the churchyard, and as they touched the wall, the other funeral, the coffin and the bearers and all, vanished as though the earth had swallowed it. They wondered at this, but they said that they had come to bury the head, and that they would bury the head. So they lifted the coffin over the wall, and came to the place where the grave was open, and there they buried the head as the young lad had asked when he was dying. So it was for a time. But after some months another man of the family died, and they opened the grave again, and what should they find there but two coffins, and in one coffin was the head and in the other the body, so that in the end the lad had his wish, and rested, head and body and all, in the grave of his fathers.'

As Peig was telling this tale I watched her, in admiration of her fine, clean-cut face, with the dark expressive eyes that change with the changing humours of her talk, all framed in her shawl that kept falling back from her head as she moved her arms in sweeping gestures, only to be caught and replaced above her brow with a twitch of the hand. As she finished, a gust of wind came down the chimney and drove the smoke out into the room.

'Burning and destruction on you for a chimney!' she cried, running to the backdoor and flinging it open to make a draught to carry the choking smoke out into the air. 'I always know the way the wind is blowing in this house,' she said, returning to the fire, 'for if it comes one way, do what I will the smoke fills the room, and there is nothing that will cure the chimney of that trick. And you're not used to it as we are.'

'I'm used to worse things,' I said, 'for you would wonder

if you saw a day of fog in London, when the clouds fall and the smoke of the city mixes with them, and you can't see your hand before your face in the darkness all day long, and the taste of that fog is bitter in the throat.'

'Ah, but the people of London are rich, and they can find ways to be out of the fog; not like the people of the Island, for they are bitter poor, and they are in an island of the sea as in a prison, and must take the weather and the world as it comes to them, with nothing to make their lives soft and easy like those that are free in the great world.'

'You say that, Peig,' said I, 'but it isn't true at all, for there are more people poor in London, poorer than any on the Island. There are men walking the streets now, living under the mercy of the world, and with nobody to help them, and in the winter they shiver in the cold of night without proper clothes or food.'

'Well, that is the way of the world as God made it in the beginning, for it was ordained that there should be rich and poor, and the rich cannot live without the poor, nor the poor without the rich.'

'But there are some that say now that there is no necessity for the world to be like that, and if the money in the world were divided up among all the people, all could live easily, and there would be neither rich nor poor.'

'Don't believe them, Bláheen; for that plan was tried once and we all know what came of it.'

'When was it tried?' I asked, 'and what came of it? For I never heard that it was tried yet.'

'It was this way. There was a good king once. The people liked him well, but they liked the queen, his wife, even better. For all she wished at all times was to keep the poor people up. And she was always complaining, asking why it was that the poor people didn't get fair play to lift them up out of their poverty. One day she spoke to the king. "I hope, O king," she said, "that you will do something for me, and give the poor people fair play." "Very well, my queen," said he, "you shall have your desire." She was very pleased then, but perhaps she wasn't so pleased afterwards. The king made proclamation that certain things should be done, that everyone should be put in a good way and be able to manage for himself.

'It wasn't long till the poor people were getting in a good way, and in a few years they wouldn't be at the trouble to buy or sell anything. And one day it came to pass that there wasn't a potato to be bought in any market. So the royal household was left without a potato for dinner that day. When it was dinner-time and they sat to table, the queen saw no potatoes coming. "What's this?" said she. "Isn't there a potato for my dinner to-day?" "Well, if you haven't got a potato," said the king, "you have your will. You wouldn't be satisfied till the poor got fair play, and now, when they have their own way, they don't trouble to do anything for you or for me. You ought to be satisfied." "O, if that's the way of it," said the queen, "you'll have to put a stop to this work. I must have potatoes for my dinner." So the king had to rein in the poor again, and bring them under subjection. And then the queen was satisfied.'

Having delivered this convincing refutation, from the world of fairy-tale, of the futility of the equal distribution of wealth, Peig rose from her stool on the floor, and, 'Well, Bláheen,' she said, 'we've been a long while talking, and people will be saying of me that I do nothing but sit and tell tales, and it's time you were going home to your supper.'

'It is,' I answered, and we went to the door and looked out. The sun was going down into the western sea, and its rays struck across on to the mainland. Some days

before there had been violent rain, and the watercourses
everywhere were still running full. Away up on the side
of Sliabh an Iolair, above Dunquin, a cataract could be
seen flashing white in the light of the evening sun.

'Do you see that fall?' she said. 'It was in a house below
that fall I lived when I was a girl, till it was time for me
to go into service. And I was married at seventeen. You
wouldn't see anywhere a merrier girl than I was till that
time, for it is youth that has the light foot and the happy
heart. But since the time I was married I have never
known a day that I was entirely happy. My husband was
a sick man most of his days, and then he died and left me,
and I brought up my children to read and write, and
there never were children with cleverer heads for their
books; but there was no place for them in Ireland, and
they have all gone to America but one, and soon he too
will be gone, and I shall be alone in the end of my life.
But it is God's will and the way of the world, and we must
not complain.' And she threw her shawl over her head,
and turned back into the darkening house.

GOBNAIT

THE night had fallen, and I picked my way cautiously down the broken tracks to the lower village, skirting a chasm here, stumbling over a stone there, and flashing an electric torch to guide my steps among the dangers of the way. I turned at last by a *púicín*, one of the huts of beehive shape which the islanders build to keep their tools in, descendants in a right line from the ancient dwellings of the hermit. A light came out of the doorway of the house in front of me, and I went in.

This is the house of Seán Eoghain, one of the Dunlevys, a magnificent figure of an old man like one of the heroes of Irish story. He stands still, tall and vigorous, though he is an old age pensioner, and works all day long in the field with unremitting energy. A great nose juts like a rock out of his furrowed face, between one open and one drooping eye, above a big mouth out of which, when he speaks, there comes a tremendous roar of sound that almost deafens the hearer. This voice Tomás is accustomed to call 'barrabua na Féinne', the triumph horn of the Fenians, and indeed it has more of the clamour of a great horn blowing for battle than of the sound of a human throat.

As I come in he is sitting by the fire, his son's child on his knee, that mighty organ of speech muted to the timbre of a lullaby as he soothes the little creature to sleep. My entrance breaks the spell, for he raises his voice in welcome.

'By the lovely devil,' he says with a favourite oath, 'it's a good sight to see you under the shelter of my rafters, Bláheen. Take the chair by the fire, and Méiní will give you a cup of tea.'

'That I will and welcome,' says Méiní.

'Don't be troubling yourself, Méiní,' I say. 'I have just come from my supper, and if I didn't drink enough tea there it's my own fault.'

Méiní returns to the settle from which she had risen to make the tea, and I take the chair by the hearth.

'Perhaps you are right,' says Seán, 'for it's that same tea has ruined the people's health. I remember the day when there was no tea on the Island, and no knowledge of it either, or of sugar or white bread. In those days we lived on bread of Indian meal and milk and fish and potatoes, and there wasn't a man on the Island that didn't carry a whole set of teeth to the grave. But now the teeth rot in the mouths of the children before they are fully grown, and it's tea and sugar and white bread that have done it, bad luck on them!'

Seán's daughter-in-law, who is one of the two village schoolmistresses, was sitting by the table, and, 'Well, Seán,' said she, 'you eat white bread gladly enough yourself, and you never had your fill of sugar in your tea yet.'

'Yes, yes, yes,' he said, for it is a trick of his to repeat his words three times, 'we must go with the world even when it takes the wrong path, but the old way was the better.'

The door opened in the middle of this argument, and Gobnait, Peats Sheámuis's wife, came in and sat on the settle by Méiní. She is a strongly built woman of forty, with a sallow face under dark, untidy hair, and the bright quick eyes of a teller of tales. Seán turns to her, and 'Gobnait,' says he, 'haven't you a tale to tell that would put this child to sleep?'

'I would be ashamed to be telling tales in front of Bláheen,' she answers, 'for he has heard all the tales of the world, and he'd find no taste on the tale I tell to amuse the children by the fire at night.'

'Why, Gobnait, that is just the kind of tale I like, for I'm tired of the tales in the books, and the oldest man is

no more than a grown-up child, and why wouldn't he be
pleased with the tales that are told to children?'

'Well,' says she, 'have you ever heard the tale of Purty
deas Squarey?'

'I have not. And who was Purty deas Squarey?'

'He was a dog, and you'll hear all about him in the
tale.'

'But what does Squarey mean?'

'I don't know, but that's how I always heard the name
in the tale.'

'Perhaps he was a four-cornered dog,' I suggest.

'Maybe you're right, Bláheen,' says Seán, 'for that's
the meaning of "square" in English, and that's the word
that's in it.'

'Well, whether or no, that's the name he had,' says
Gobnait, 'and he was a good dog too, as you'll hear in the
tale. Once upon a time there was a king,' she began, and
falling into the steady voice of the story-teller she began
upon the tale.

As she sat there, pouring out the tale in a steady voice,
her fingers were not idle. The parish priest and the curate
were coming to the Island within a few days to hold
stations, to say Masses in the school and hear confessions.
They would catechize the children, and the little ones
must be neatly dressed for the great occasion.

Gobnait was making a dress for Máirín, Seán's grand-
child, and, as her lips formed the phrases of the tale, her
fingers were busy sewing hard at the stuff that lay across
her knees. The others made no scruple of breaking in on
her story where any occasion for approval or dissent
occurred, and after every outburst she would tranquilly
resume the interrupted thread, driving in the needle with
new emphasis, and taking up the tale again with a fresh
impulse. At last the tale ended with the triumph of
persecuted virtue, and the little girl gave a satisfied sigh

and fell asleep. Her mother picked her up and carried her into the inner room to bed.

I dived into my pocket and produced a notebook. 'I would like to have that tale down in writing,' I said.

'Well, well, well,' said Seán, 'isn't it an odd thing that a scholar from the city of London should want to write down a silly little tale for children?'

'Nevertheless, if Gobnait can tell it again slowly, I will try to write it down.'

So Méiní lit a candle at my elbow to throw light on my book, and setting my chair against Gobnait, and resting the book on the table, I prepared to follow her voice with flying pencil.

'Once upon a time there was a king,' she began again. 'It's often there was and there will be for ever. He was married and he had one daughter when his wife died; and he married again and he had one daughter by that wife, and she was not as beautiful as the king's daughter. The stepmother was jealous of the king's daughter, and she was always scheming how she should put her to death.'

'Now isn't it wonderful, Bláheen,' broke in Seán, 'that in the old time all stepmothers were bad women. Why was that, do you think?'

'I don't know,' I said, 'for there are good and bad stepmothers just as there is good and bad in everything else. But there wouldn't be a tale if the stepmother wasn't wicked, and I expect that's why it is.'

'Maybe,' he said. 'Go on, Gobnait.'

'So she went one day to the old wizard and asked him how she could put the king's daughter to death. He said that he knew quite well; she must pretend to be ill, and that she could not be cured unless the king's daughter were sent to the Well of the Heads to fetch three bottles of water. She came home and lay down on her bed. The king went to see her, and asked her was there anything that would cure her.

'She said there was; to send his daughter to the Well of the Heads for three bottles of water. "I won't send my daughter there," he said, "unless she's willing to go." His daughter said that she would go and welcome. So she got herself ready for the road; she fetched a basket and put in it everything she wanted for the road, and then she went to the corner of the demesne to the old woman, and the old woman gave her some food. She asked her where she was going, and she said, to the Well of the Heads for her step-mother. Off she went along the road, and she was going on till she came to a spring of water, and she sat down to eat a little food, and she hadn't been eating long when there came a robin of the Sullivan family to her. "Bit or bite for my chicks that are in the hole in the wall for a quarter of the year." "Sit down," said she, "and eat your fill."

'Before the robin sat down she drew her tail through the well, and turned its surface to honey and its bottom to blood, and then they ate their fill. She left her enough for her chicks, and off she went and reached the Well of the Heads. She dipped a bottle in the well, and a head came up to her. "Wash and cleanse me," said the head, "and change me from hand to hand and put me on yonder flagstone." "That's why I've come," she said, and she washed him and dried him with her towel, and the head leapt from her hand and went on the flagstone.

'She dipped the second bottle, and another head rose up to her. "Wash and cleanse me and change me from hand to hand and set me on yonder flagstone." "God save your soul, that's why I'm here." She washed and cleansed him and dried him with her towel, and the head leapt from her hand and went over on the flagstone.'

'They were great leppers, those heads,' said Seán, 'and how did they do it without legs?'

'How should I know? That's how I always heard the tale. So she dipped the third bottle, and the third head rose up to her. "Wash and cleanse me and change me from hand to hand, and set me on yonder flagstone," said the third head. "God save your soul, that's why I'm here," said she, and she washed and cleansed him, and dried him with her towel, and the head leapt from her hand and went over on the flagstone.

'Then she fixed up her bottles, and settled them in her basket, and she was going off when one of the heads spoke. "What gift will you give her?" said he to the other heads. "To be more beautiful than she is, when she goes home." "And what gift will you give her?" said the other head. "That nobody shall ever get the upper hand of her." "And what gift will you give her?" said he to the third head. "I will give her every time she combs her head to comb white silver down out of it."

'Off she went, and she went to the little old woman, and she welcomed her a hundred and a thousand times for joy that she had come safe home again. She washed and cleansed herself, and she combed her head in the old woman's lap, and she left a good covering of silver on the lap when she had finished combing.'

'That money was easy got,' commented Seán.

'She came home then. When her stepmother saw her come home safe and sound, she wasn't too pleased. She went to the old wizard again. "There now, where shall I send her now?" "Send your own daughter there." She came home and told her daughter to go off to the Well of the Heads to fetch her three bottles of water. Off went the daughter, and she was going on till she came to the spring. She sat down to eat by the well, and the robin of the Sullivan family came to her. "Bit or bite," said the robin, "or hard crumb of bread for my chicks that are in the hole in the wall for a quarter of the year." "I haven't enough for myself." The robin drew her tail through the spring, and made the surface of blood and the bottom of honey, and hardly could she eat for the bread was choking her.

'Off she went then, and she came to the Well of the Heads; she dipped a bottle and a head rose up to her. "Wash and cleanse me and change me from hand to hand and set me on yonder flagstone." "Hump under hump on me," said she, "if I do that." She dipped the second bottle and another head rose up to her. "Wash and cleanse me and change me from hand to hand and set me on yonder flagstone." "May I break my leg," said she, "if I do it." She dipped the third bottle, and the third head rose up. "Wash and cleanse me and change me from hand to hand, and set me on yonder flagstone." "May I be uglier than I am if I do it," said she.

'She put the bottles back in the basket and off with her. They considered what gifts they should give her. "Hump under hump," said one of the heads. "A broken leg," said the second head. "To be uglier than she is," said the third head.'

'Bad luck to her, it's well she earned the hump and the broken leg and the ugliness!' said Méiní.

'Off home she went, and when she came home she fell on the threshold and broke her leg, and she spent a time in bed, and when she got up again she was uglier than before and had a hump under a hump on her back.

'Her mother was very angry, and she went to the old wizard again. She told him that she was making the king's daughter more beautiful than before, and her own daughter uglier than before. "Don't mind that," said the wizard. "I'll put her in a place that will keep her. Pretend you're ill, and that nothing will cure you but to send the king's daughter to such and such a mill to get a bag of wheat ground; and nobody in the world ever came back from that mill." She told this to the king. "I won't send her unless she wants to go," he said. He asked his daughter whether she would go to such and such a mill. She said she would go. She got herself ready for the road, everything she needed, and she didn't forget to go to the little old woman with her basket. She gave her a little cock, and told her to put him in her basket.

'When she had come to the mill, there was nobody there but two lads. They said that it was rather late to grind the wheat, that she must wait till to-morrow. She asked them had they any boiling water. They said they had, and gave her a kettle of boiling water, and she made tea and everything she wanted, and laid it out ready on the table. She told the two lads to draw up their chairs and eat along with her, and they did so.

'When that was done, they were very grateful to her, and they stayed far into the night with her. They said then that they could not take her with them, and she must stay in the mill till morning. Off they went then, and it wasn't long till a tall, black man came down the chimney to her. "Stretch out your long white legs beside my long black legs." "I'll do it," she said, "if you'll make me a golden cupboard." He wasn't long making it. "Stretch out your long white legs beside my long black legs." "I'll do it if you'll make me a golden dresser." "Stretch out your long white legs beside my long black legs." "I'll do it if you'll make me a golden ladder." Yerra, he hadn't put the last nail in the ladder when the little cock flapped his wings and crowed, and the tall, black man went out through the chimney.'

'That was a clever girl; she wasn't long getting her gold furniture. It's a pity she didn't get a golden house to put it in before the cock crowed,' said Seán.

'When the lads came in the morning they were delighted to find her alive; they ground her wheat and tied up her parcels for her. When the stepmother saw her back again she nearly fell into a faint. She went back to the old wizard, and he told her to send her own daughter there. When she came home she sent her own daughter to the mill to grind wheat.

'She went off to the mill, and she gave no greeting to anybody, but she had a surly look, and when she came to the mill the lads said they couldn't grind her corn till morning. She asked them for a cup of boiling water and got it. She made a cup of tea for herself and never gave a thought to anybody else. They went away then and left her alone. She wasn't long till the tall, black man came down the chimney. "Stretch out your long white legs beside my long black legs." "I couldn't," said she, "for I have a hump under a hump." "Stretch out your long white legs beside my long black legs." "I couldn't, for my leg's broken." "Stretch out your long white legs beside my long black legs." "I couldn't for I'm uglier than ever I was." All he did was to gulp her up in his mouth and fly out of the chimney with her.'

'Going without returning on her, for she was a bad bargain for any man,' said Méiní.

'When the lads came in the morning there was no trace of her to be found. They ground the wheat, and sent the horse home with a message to her mother. When the king saw that the other daughter was gone, he said to himself that the stepmother meant to put his own daughter to death.'

'Ambaist, he might have seen that long before,' said Seán, 'if he'd had his wits about him.'

'So he married her far and far away from home. When she was married a year she had a little daughter, and her husband sent for her stepmother to look after her. When she came she struck her with a magic wand, and turned her into a deer, and sent her out into the park among the other deer, and put an old woman in her shape into the bed in her place. But when the Prince went to tend the deer on the morrow, he saw a strange deer among them, and she wouldn't eat any food, but was fawning about him. That was very well until the night came, and she had a little dog that was called Purty deas Squarey, and she spoke to the dog in the night through the window. "Are you in bed, Purty deas Squarey?" "I am not in bed," said Purty. "Where is the baby?" "She's in the cradle." "Where is the master?" "He's in the parlour." "Where is the old hag?" "She's in the corner."

'Off she went till the next night came. "Are you in bed, Purty deas Squarey?" "I am not in bed," said Purty. "Where is the baby?" "She's in the cradle." "Where is the master?" "He's in the parlour." "Where is the old hag?" "She's in the corner."

'But the servant was listening the next night, and he went to the Prince and told him about the deer that came to the window at night and spoke to the little dog. "Never mind that," he said, "till to-night." When the edge of the evening came, they put a piece of leather on the dog's muzzle. They left the window open, but when the night came she came to the window and she called to Purty, and of course Purty didn't answer her. So she came in through the window. And the first rush she made was to the cradle, and there she fawned upon the child. They caught her then, and her husband asked her what would cure her now. She said that if they cast the Holy Water of Christmas Day and the Holy Water of Easter Sunday on her she would be as well as ever she was. He sent for the Holy Water and it was cast upon her, and she was cured then and became a woman again. They seized the step-mother, and made a great fire of turf, and put her in the middle of the fire, and she was burnt and consumed. That is my tale, and if there is a lie in it, be it so.'

I scribbled down the last words, and let the pencil drop from my cramped fingers. 'Thank you, Gobnait,' I said, 'that's a fine tale, and they are lucky children that you tell such tales to.'

'Well, well, well,' broke in Seán, 'it's a good tale enough, but we wouldn't have called that a tale at all in the old times. Devil take my soul, it's long before I'd put a tale like that in comparison with the long Fenian stories we used to tell. It was only the other day that I had all the old tales in my mind, and I could have spent the night telling them to you without a word out of its place in any tale. But now I couldn't tell a tale of them. And do you know what has driven them out of my head?'

'Well, I suppose you're losing your memory,' I said.

'No, it isn't that, for my memory is as good as it ever was for other things. But it's Tomás has done it, for he has books and newspapers and he reads them to me, and the little tales one after another, day after day, in the books and the newspapers, have driven the old stories out of my head. But maybe I'm little the worse for losing them.'

Here, I thought, was the clash of the two traditions, the oral and the printed, vividly present in the figure of that heroic old man. Twenty years ago his mind was alive with antique memories, and in him, and in men like him, the old stable world endured still as it had endured for centuries. But now the fatal drip of printer's ink has obliterated the agelong pattern, and it is only by a glint of colour here, a salient thread there, in the dulled material, that we who strive to reconstitute something of the intricate harmony wrought into the original fabric can imagine to ourselves the bright hues and gay lines of the forgotten past. The world has turned to another way of life, and no passion of regret can revive a dying memory. What on that Island has to-day been experience to me will to-morrow be history as remote as Troy and Nineveh and Ur of the Chaldees. We can preserve a little of that tradition in the ink that has destroyed it. But the reality of the tradition is passing from us now, and I can only think that the world is poorer for its passing.

THE SORROWFUL SLOPE

THE two sides of the Island, slanted different ways, have correspondingly a difference of character. The southern slope, looking towards the bay and the land, falls gently and deliberately, deciding only at the last moment, as it were, to have done with it and break in cliff to a sheltered sea. The northern side, turned to the open Atlantic, drops at once down shelving slopes of scant grass that end upon gigantic cliffs fantastically worn by the caprice of the water into vast bays or narrow gullies, at the points of which sharp rocks stand up, or battered reefs run out into the waves. Along this slope you walk at a sharp angle to the hill, following the tracks of rabbits and sheep, and look nervously down on the fangs of the sea laid bare and white upon the rocks so far below. Strange things may happen here, as the dizzy height lays a gradual spell upon the brain.

I was walking one summer day along a sheep-track just above the line where the grass merges into rock, going with an easy and certain step, and looking idly out to the horizon, along which a moveless city of white cloud stood piled to the sky. Suddenly, half-way down the cliff a raven detached itself from the rock-face, and with a hoarse cry flapped clumsily to the water's edge. Startled, I withdrew my eyes from the distance and looked down, and, looking, was mastered by the horror of the naked depth under my feet. My brain swam, my feet trembled on the track, and, with knees giving under me, I fell prone, desperately clutching with weak fingers at the slippery grass. And so on hands and knees I crawled ignominiously back along the path I had trodden so confidently a few moments before.

As I went, I remembered a story of the Skelligs. From the side of the Great Skellig a point of rock juts out over the sea, with the mark of a cross inscribed on its extremity. It is a piece of devotion to crawl out along this rock and kiss the cross. An Englishman, they say, once attempted this feat in mockery of the people's devotion. But the vengeance of Heaven overtook him half-way, and, slipping on the rock, he went down into the sea. There used to be a proverb on the opposite mainland: ' "More Water!" arsan Sasanach agus é báth'—' "More water!" cried the drowning Protestant'—and the interpretation of this was that he took so long in falling through the air that he prayed to the water to hasten to meet him and end his misery. Thinking fearfully of this I, lately come from London, prayed to all that was Irish in me to save all that was English from that horrible descent, and my prayer was heard. I reached a less precipitous slope, and lay there panting till the causeless fear had passed. I was careful ever after how I went that way again.

It is to this abrupt escarpment of the Island that the angry Atlantic brings its victims in days and nights of storm. And there are many memories of wrecks of old and recent date; of sudden knockings at doors in the night and the appearence of dripping bewildered men, speaking strange languages and asking and receiving shelter; of unexpected relief coming out of the sea in days of difficulty. It was this uncovenanted bounty of the sea that brought the Island through the Great Famine.

'In the bad times,' says the tale, 'the Great Blasket had little to boast about any more than any other place, though it is to be said that no one died there of famine or hunger, praise to God. When those years began, the first year of them a man was on the crest of the hill in this Island. He saw coming to him out of the north-east through the the bay a two-masted ship, and he marked, from the way she was driving, that she was in a poor way with few people to guide her. He had an eye following her for the great part of an afternoon, and he recognized that there was nobody steering her, for she was making no course at all, but going as the wind and tide cast her. Darkness and the late hour were coming on him and he must needs go home. He related to the people of his kindred that such a ship was in the bay to the north, and that she seemed to him to be driving at random, and maybe if any should be out early in the morning that judging from the direction of the wind they would find her cast up on the beach in the morning.

'So it was. They kept an eye out for her, and especially the man who had seen her first, for he never went to sleep that night. Early up though he was, there were others as early. They searched all the nearer beaches ever and always till they had gone a third part of the Island, and then they found her cast up, body and bones, on one of the beaches. They went down, and there was still weather and working in the sea, and a great tide running and storm in a like measure. She was being bruised and broken before their eyes, and they could do no good with her, for they had no calm. They had to go up and leave the beach that day.

'On the day and the morrow it was calmer weather. They looked about and they saw the sea full of yellow lumps like butter so far as their eyes could reach. Some of it was thrown up on the beach where the vessel was, some in all the beaches eastward from it. A few of the boats put out and they were picking up the lumps. The vessel had a cargo of palm oil, a good thing worth money, but the islanders didn't know that it was so. Had they known they would have gone to more trouble about it than they did. The vessel had no bolt of iron in all her frame, but only bolts of brass and copper. They picked up a good share of these while they lasted, and they got a good price of gold for them when they sold them, for people came oversea to buy from them.

'When the palm-oil season was past, and the last of it picked up but for an odd lump going on the tide, they faced for the beach where was the body of the ship. One man would find a brass bolt as long as himself, and another a bolt of copper. They were finding these bolts for the greater part of the year at the low tides, so that they worked through the first year of the Famine with no loss by means of this ship. When they had picked up the sails, spars, and timber, and turned them into money they got good money out of them all. That was the first year of the Famine, and they didn't do so badly.

'The next year not a plant grew up through the earth either, and the past year didn't serve their turn. They needed some other fortune to come their way. Not much of that year had gone by when in the spring there came another two-masted ship to them drifting before the weather, for her steering-gear was stricken out of her. She was cast up below the houses on a white shore of sand that is there, and that is an evil shore on a stormy day for saving anybody that is out to sea from it.

'Some of that crew too were not saved, though the islanders did their best for them. They brought in some of them, but others slipped out of their hands. She was laden with wheat. When the vessel split, the wheat went out in a white foaming mass. A great deal of it came to them into the clefts about the Island. They gathered it up as eagerly as they could, for they knew well there was food in it, whatever was the case with the palm oil the year before. They picked up and dried and put in store so much of it that they worried through the year with it, so that the second year of the Famine wasn't so bad for them either. There would have been little to say of them if it hadn't been for these two chances that came their way.

The third year they worried through too, putting it past them though no chance came their way that year; but God's help was near them, for there was a change for the better the year after, and the world has been getting better and better with every day since till to-day, praise be to God.'

The place of the first of these fortunate wrecks is commemorated, I suppose, in the name of one of the Island beaches, Cladach an Chopuir, the beach of the Copper. This fashion of naming places after notorious events is responsible for much of the nomenclature of the Island. There is a slope of land, at the point where the northern front of the Island turns to form the western face, that has for name An Leaca Chlúch, and this, Tomás maintains, is a corruption of the older Leaca Dhúch, the Sorrowful Slope. This name is derived from a dreadful event which happened in the patch of sea immediately below the slope. As you cross the ridge leading to this place, Mám na Leacan, you look down on a quiet stretch of water under the cliff, the sea-passage into which is restless with little islands and sunken rocks and sudden swirls of tide

'There was no patch of sea,' says Tomás, 'so noted for fish in the old days as this slope; every kind of fish, whether taken with rod or net. In those days there was no point of the compass in County Kerry but boats would be coming from it to fish here, they would be at it day and night without ceasing till they had the boat full of every kind of fish that you could take. They used to fish with the seine net in the night and with the rod by day. They were thus always keeping good watch to get fit weather to go into it, for it was an ill passage that led to it, with swirls of tide and sunken rocks. A fine night came, with no swell or wind, and the boats were coming towards this place for the night like black crows. Every one of them made the passage west without fear, and they fell to fishing, and it wasn't long till the night was rising and getting up with a swell on the rocks, showers came out of the north-west, and wind with them. The wind hadn't been blowing long when it raised a sea against the land. They all fell to getting in their nets, and they were making their best speed of hand and foot. A good share of those who were at work first came safe, but the blast swept away so many boats that there were sixteen widows when morning came. Though this slope carried off so many, it had to pay for it in the end, for the boats were not so set on going into it as they had been.'

'OUR LADY OF THE ROSARY'

THE passage in which this tragedy occurred was no
doubt the way in from the sea between the long rock
known as Carraig Fhada and the Rocks of the Road, the
ea-space between Beiginis and the reefs. This same passage had been the inlet to a more terrible disaster in the
far past, when the battered Armada ships came in to
shelter among the islands from the rage of the open
Atlantic. Looking to-day upon that angry confusion of
rocks and sea, we can hardly imagine how the great
unmanageable galleons could have found a way through
the open and concealed dangers of that passage. I remember a day, a few years ago, on which some distant storm
far off in the Atlantic sent in the last of its waves to batter
the islands. There was something very dreadful in the
sudden rising of the sea on a day of calm airs, for the great
rollers appeared to be driving in on us by an uncommuni-
cated volition of their own, independent of the will of the
sky. Long before they reached the line of reefs that run
out from the point of the Island their heads began to
topple over in foam, and then they would cast themselves on the rocks, tower up in innumerable fountains to
the sky, and at last in their fall bury the black rocks in a
white confusion of foam. The long shape of Carraig Fhada
would disappear entirely, and then gradually emerge here
and there through veils of streaming snow, only to be
buried again as another wall of water crashed down on it
from the sky. Between this island in travail and the Rocks
of the Road the long unbroken surges hastened in, to
shatter themselves at last on the front of Beiginis. The
white gulls fluttered over this witch's cauldron, indifferent
to the trouble of the water, and black cormorants, flying
low and fast with their wonted air of messengers

dispatched upon a journey that brooks no delay, shot arrow-like through the hanging walls of foam.

In sight of this wrecking sea one came to realize that only very desperate and very brave men could have dared the passage of the reefs. But the men of the Armada were brave beyond question (though they were commanded by one who was possibly a craven and certainly a fool), and they had good reason to be desperate. For months they had known every extremity of the sea, and endured the last agonies of battle, starvation, and disease. After the week's fighting in the English Channel, the night of the fire-ships in Calais Roads, and the fatal fight off Gravelines, they had turned north, and, shaking off at last their persistent enemies, had come out into the Atlantic, between the Orkneys and the Shetlands. Medina Sidonia's last order was prophetic of their fate. 'The course that is to be held', he had written, 'is to the NNE., until you be found under 61 degrees and a half; and then to take great heed lest you fall upon the island of Ireland, for fear of the harm that may happen to you upon that coast.'

The harm that happened to so many of the great ships upon that coast is written in history, though the whole pitiful story has never been fully told. They had come out into the open sea on the 9th and 10th of August, and had been beating about the Atlantic through all that month and well into September, the helpless victims of a series of cyclones which drove them inflexibly in upon the open harbours and unforgiving cliffs of that dreaded island of Ireland. A little company of ships, the chance companions of the storm, ran in upon the Kerry coast on the 11th of September. One of these was the flagship of Martinez de Recalde, Admiral of the whole Armada, who had a bitter knowledge of Corcaguiney, for he had commanded the fleet which had landed the Spanish force doomed to slaughter in the fort of Smerwick a few short years before.

The ironic storm drove them in on the islands and then snatched them out again into the sea, and once more changing its purpose brought them back to the land.

On the 15th, Recalde's ship, the *St. John*, and another ship, the *St. John Baptist*, of the Squadron of Castile, both great galleons of 1,050 and 750 tons, came together round Inis Tuaisceart, and made for the anchorage between the Great Blasket and Beiginis. They dared not attempt the passage between Beiginis and the mainland, for fear of the cliffs of Dunquin and the projecting promontory of Dún Mór. So they risked the desperate hazard of the space, only a ship's length in width, between Carraig Fhada and the reefs. They came through somehow between the spouting rocks, and anchored on the sandy bottom between the islands. Recalde sent in a boat to the mainland for water, and its crew fell into the hands of the English who lined the cliffs. Another boat had better success, and brought off the water of which they had so desperate a need.

For some days they rode at anchor there, and were joined on the 21st by the *St. Mary of the Rosary*, coming in by the land passage, and another ship, the *St. John of Ragusa*, which had lost its mainmast and ran in under the foresail, that was blown to shreds as she made the passage. The *St. Mary of the Rosary* too had lost all her sails but the foresail, and as the tide came in from the south-east she dragged her anchor, and, drifting across the Sound, struck upon a rock under the cliffs and went down with all her crew. One man only, John Anthony of Genoa, the pilot's son, came to shore, and was immediately seized by the pitiless watchers stationed there.

He was examined in Dingle, and he had a strange story to tell. His deposition stands on record in the State Papers. 'The Spanish King's base son', he said, speaking of the Prince of Asculo, a natural son of Philip II, 'came in the

company of the Duke of Medina Sidonia's ship, called the
galleon of St. Martin, of 1,000 tons; but at Calais, when
Sir Francis Drake came near them, this prince went in a
pinnace to the shore, and before his return the Duke was
driven to cut his cables and let go his anchors and to
depart, whereby the Prince could not recover that ship,
but came into the ship called *Our Lady of the Rosary* with
Don Pedro, Don Diego, Don Francisco, and others. His
ship struck on the rocks in the Sound of Blasquets, when a
captain killed the pilot, this examinate's father, saying
it was by treason. There were 4,000 killed in fight off
Calais, and 1,000 drowned in two ships. All the company,
including the King of Spain's base-born son, the Prince
of Asculo, were drowned on Tuesday last, excepting only
this examinate.'

It is like the scene at the opening of Shakespeare's
Tempest; the royal passenger at the mercy of the roarers
that care nothing for the name of king, the confusion on
the ship in its extremity, and the outcry upon the pilot:

We are merely cheated of our lives by drunkards:
This wide-chapp'd rascal—would thou might'st lie drowning
The washing of ten tides!

And so they did. Ten tides and more than ten tides must
have washed those broken bodies on the fanged rocks of
that iron-bound coast. And of all that tragedy, all that
remains in the people's memory is the fate of this very
Prince of Asculo. Near the schoolhouse in Dunquin you
may still see a grave which the people call 'The grave of
the King's son of Spain'. Of all the others who died on
that day no record remains, for they lacked the glamour
even of illegitimate royalty to keep their names alive on
the lips of men.

This wrecking of *Our Lady of the Rosary* happened with
the turn of the ebb at two of the afternoon. At four of the

clock on the same afternoon the *St. John of Ragusa*, Fernando Horra's ship, came in and asked for help, which could not be given her because of the violence of the gale. On the next day, the 22nd, Recalde sent a boat, and the men and treasure were taken off, but it proved impossible to salve the guns. This ship too went down somewhere in the Sound. On the 23rd a desperate attempt was made to clear the islands, but the wind fell and the ships began to drift with the tide towards the land. They were forced to anchor again. Night fell, and with night a wind rose in the south-east, and began to crowd the ships on the islands. They commended themselves to the Blessed Virgin and drove at the reefs once more. It was a dark night, the sky muffled with clouds, out of which a heavy rain was pouring, and the sea was rising on the rocks. But more by luck than skill they cleared the islands and stood out into the Atlantic.

For the next few days they staggered about the sea, the uncertain wind driving them this way and that, the sick and famished crew hardly able to haul upon the ropes as the ship came about, the guns in the ballast rolling from side to side with the send of the waves, and great seas coming on board between the high castles at prow and stern. Then at last they found their way home to Spain, and Recalde took to his bed, his heart broken with the shame of that great enterprise gone awry, and in two days died in silence.

It is a matter of wonder that no tradition remains among the people of this huge calamity. The galleons had ridden off the Island for days, two of them had gone down in the Sound, the cliffs were crowded with spectators looking down on the great hulks, with their patched sides and the dishonoured gilding of their stern galleries, their broken masts and tattered sails, and their spectral company eaten with disease, hollow with hunger, and half-crazed with the agony of past experience and present fear. We have seen that a real tradition of the King's son survives, but for the rest, the mercy of oblivion had hidden the manner of their calamity until the curious research of to-day disinterred it from the records of England and the yellowing papers of Simancas. The people kept their tears for their own disasters, and the sixteen widows of the Sorrowful Slope are better remembered than the hundreds that went down with *Our Lady of the Rosary*.

PIERCE FERRITER

POPULAR tradition is indeed a thing capricious and unaccountable. It remembers, but not as history remembers, seizing upon elements of character and event that the folk mind can assimilate to its own mode of thought, and ruthlessly casting away all beside, confusing times and characters, and building its own timeless world out of the wreck of history. Thus I have heard a line of song that told of 'Patrick Sarsfield who gave laws to the Irish in the days of Queen Elizabeth'; and another hero of the seventeenth century, Pierce Ferriter, whose home was in this country-side, has suffered a curious change, paying for his survival in memory by the surrender of most of the characteristics which so nobly distinguished the living man.

I heard the name of Pierce Ferriter on the Island for the first time in a strange way. We were sitting in the King's kitchen one night, talking idly about everything and nothing, when the door opened and a man came rather wearily in. At his entrance a complete silence fell on the company, and the King's son, getting up from the settle, went into the inner room and brought out a number of boxes of rough white deal. 'Will these do?' he asked. 'They will,' said the other, and taking the boxes turned on his heel and was gone without another word. For a few minutes a heavy silence hung over the company, and then one spoke, another answered, and the idle, indifferent talk went on. It was not till the next morning that I understood the meaning of this scene.

The day broke in rain, and after breakfast I sat by the fire reading, while the day's supply of bread was baking in the pot oven. At a sudden exclamation from the King's daughter I rose and glanced out of the window. A little

procession was coming from the top of the village, and
from every house, as it passed, the men, women, and
children came out to join it. The King's daughter took
the pot from the fire, placed it carefully by the smouldering
sods, and, turning to me, said: 'It is the funeral. Will you
come?'

A few words told me all. A new-born baby had died,
and the father had come to us the night before for wood
to make the coffin. He walked now at the head of the
procession through the rain, with the little box that he had
knocked together from that raw, unhallowed wood under
his arm. We too went out and joined the company. It
wound through the scattered houses of the village, always
increasing; the men wearing their hats of felt, the women
with their shawls drawn close about their heads, and all
in a speechless trance of sorrow or respect. The rain swept
across the Sound in long veils drifting over the dead calm
of the sea, and the Island seemed as though shut off from
the whole world by those shifting walls of water under the
heavy sky.

We turned into a little promontory of the cliff beyond
the houses, and stopped in an unkempt space of dank,
clinging grass, with stones scattered over it here and
there. A man with a spade had dug a shallow grave, and
there, amid the sobs of the women and the muttered
prayers of the whole assembly, the father with a weary
gesture laid away his child. The earth was shovelled back,
closing with hardly a sound about the little box, a few
prayers were said, and then we all turned listlessly away,
leaving the lonely, unfledged soul to its eternity, and
drifting back ourselves, the willing or unwilling prisoners
of time, through the rough tracks among the houses. It
was now about eleven o'clock, the turn of the day, and as
we went the mists broke, blue spaces grew in the sky, and
the returning sun seemed to wither up the flying rain-

squalls between the Island and the mainland, and to give us back to the world again. The scattering groups fell to talking once more, and life, which for so brief a moment had hung suspended over that naked promontory above the grey water, took up again its customary course in quiet sunlight over the sparkling sea.

Tomás's house is in the lower village not far from this unconsecrated graveyard, and I went in with him to talk awhile, and shake off, if I could, the oppression of the doings of that morning. He kicked aside the cat, which had the best place before the fire, and I sat down on a little stool with my feet to the turf, watching the smoke curl up and disappear in the great open chimney. He took his seat on the settle and began to talk of the place we had just left. There, he said, the islanders had been accustomed to bury suicides and unbaptized children; a sad association, I thought, of those who had known nothing and those who had known too much of life.

'I remember well,' he went on, 'how once, when we were digging a grave, we found shaped stones below the earth, and there were the marks of lime on the stones. It was said that Pierce Ferriter had his castle there, a place that he could fly to when the chase was too hot upon his heels.'

'Pierce Ferriter?' I cried. 'That would be the poet?'

'The poet it was, and, beyond being a poet, he was many other things too. He had done many deeds out of the way, things that didn't please the King and his people. So the watch was out after him, and before they caught him in the end, and hanged him, he had many a shift to keep his feet free of them. They did their best to come up with him, but he was too clever for them for a good while. He had this castle built on the brink of the cliff, and he used to live in it; but when the chase was too near to him he had another place, a cave in the hill that neither deer nor eagle could come at.

'A day of the days, on an early morning of summer, he was living lightly in his castle, and he put his head out and what should he see but the guard right over against him. Terror seized him that they should be out so early in the morning, and he had no time to think of a shift. He said to himself that the best thing he could do was to yield himself up to them and take things easily. He told their captain that, if it was he they wanted, he was well pleased to go with them, for he had been too long on his keeping escaping from them, and he would rather go with them to suffer all they could do to him than live the life he had been living any longer. They were pleased enough, for they had thought he would fall to fighting with them as he had done often enough before. They agreed together, and Pierce said to them that maybe they had been out and about without food and drink too long, and that he would give orders for dinner to be made ready for them, if they wished. The captain said it was so and they had good need of it. Pierce told the girl to get dinner ready, and he bade them come along with him to the crest of the hill, where they might have a fine view while the dinner was preparing. He told them to throw away their guns and not be bothered carrying them. Finding him fine and easy in the morning they were fine and easy with him too, and did whatever he told them. They threw aside their guns, and before they went to the hill Pierce spoke aside to the girl and told her not to spare water on the guns when they were out of sight. The girl Pierce had was no fool, for if she had been he wouldn't have had her.

'Off they went, they climbed the hill and they spent a good time walking on the hill till they thought it was time for the dinner to be ready. Then they turned back to the castle. When they were drawing near to it, Pierce said that he would go in front, for the way in was rather troublesome. So he went in before them, and when he was inside there was a corner of the castle above the cliff with only room for one man at a time to go the way. The next man wouldn't know whereabouts in the castle the man in front would have stopped. When the first man came by the corner where Pierce was, Pierce thrust at him with a piece of wood and with that thrust sent him down the cliff, and the next man after him, and so with all who came in to the last man, none of them knowing where the man before had gone, till there were fifty men lying in the creek dead corpses in a heap. Pierce did well that day, but he wouldn't have been so comfortable in his castle if he had known that the pursuit was so near upon his heels.'

'Well,' said I, as the tale ended, 'that was a bad day for the soldiers.'

'It was so;' said he, 'but it would have been as bad a day for Pierce if he hadn't had his wits about him.'

'And have you any tale,' I said, 'of Pierce's cave back in the hill?'

'Yes,' he answered, 'it was there he made the verse of poetry.'

'And what verse was that?'

'Wait and you will hear it in its right place in the tale. For every tale has its order, and it's a poor story-teller that would put the end before the beginning.'

'Follow on with you then,' said I, 'and I will wait for the verse to the end.'

'Well, whenever Pierce felt the pursuit coming too close to him he would fly to this cave that was in the steepest and the worst cliff in the Island. There's many a man in the Island to-day that couldn't walk in the place where it is. However, he was often lonely in it in days of storm and wild weather. The great sea would come up to it, and he could hear the noise of the swell roaring below it. The place where this cave is is a great wide flagstone, with a

hole going into it below, and a fine uneven space within.
Six feet from it there was a great gush of spring water
running down very convenient for him. There was a
constant drip falling from the middle of the stone that
roofed it, and it was always a marvel to him why that drip
should be in the heart of the stone while all the rest of the
cave was as dry as a fox's earth. A day of the days he was
lying his length in it and this drip fell down on him, and he
made this verse that follows:

Hast Thou no pity, O God, that I lie this way,
Lonely and cold, and hardly I see the day;
The drip from the heart of the stone never stilled in my ear,
And the voice of the sea at my feet ever echoing near?'

I wrote down the verse, leaving the tales to be recorded
at another time. The day of which I speak was in the
spring of the year. The turf had been cut and laid out to
dry on the slope of the hill, and was now ready to be built
into a rick. Tomás rose, and going to the dresser at the
bottom of the kitchen by the door poured out a glass of
milk for me. I drank it, and we went out together into the
warm sun of midday. Up through the village we climbed
at the slow Island pace. For nobody ever hurries there,
the leisurely amble of the ruminating donkeys setting the
pace for the deliberate activities of the day.

Tomás's rick lies but a little way round the shoulder of
the hill, and, arrived there, I sat upon a broad stone fallen
from the base of the rick, while he built up the turf from
the little piles of sods up-ended against one another, which
covered the ground.

Long practice has made all the actions of the Island
economy unconscious, and his hands worked lightly and
certainly of themselves, while his mind and his talk still
dwelt upon Pierce Ferriter and his wild doings. For in the
people's tradition Pierce has degenerated strangely from

the gallant figure of history, the poet chieftain whose memory stands out with a kind of heroic grace from the turbulent background of the wars of '41. His poems are a strange blend of the laments and eulogies and satires of the Irish tradition and the love-lyrics of the European fashion, strangely transmuted by the alchemy of the Irish mind, which in translating never leaves anything as it finds it, but mixes inevitably a strong infusion of the native idiom and vision with whatever foreign matter comes its way. His deeds are written in the melancholy history of the seventeenth century.

> He lived a life of sturt and strife
> And died by treachery.

All this is changed once more in the simple tradition of the country-side. His actual poems are for the most part forgotten, though fragments are remembered here and there, and I have been told that even in far Donegal one of his poems has been in our day taken down from living lips. But for the most part he has become a centre for the drifting verses which have no discoverable father, and many of his actions too have decorated other heroes before the powerful magic of his personality drew them to himself. He has become the typical 'man on his keeping', the hero of a hundred evasions, a fellow of infinite resource and wile, always giving the slip to the noose which hangs waiting for him, and which will have him in the end. But, when that end comes—the gallows on the Hill of the Sheep in Killarney—his gay gallantry flashes out at the last, and he flings away his hope of life on a point of honour. A priest had given him, the tale goes, a fragment of the consecrated wafer, and promised him that while he held that holy bread under his tongue he could not die. Thrice they made to hang him, but thrice the rope broke. By the law of the gallows he was now free, but as he went away a sudden thought came to him. 'I will never live,' he cried, 'to be called the leavings of a rope,' and he turned back, and, spitting out the charmed fragment, he submitted his neck again, and now for the last time, to the strangling noose.

SEÁN Ó DUÍNNLÉ

THE Island had to wait two hundred years for another poet. They were a rough, violent people, reports Tomás, living a hard life at odds with the world, and they had little time for poetry and prayers and charms and such other childish things.

But with the dawn of the nineteenth century there was born in a house of the far-wandered family of Dunlevy a poet whose memory is still vivid among the people. It was the time of Napoleon's war, and the year that saw the birth of the poet saw also the building of the grim look-out tower which crowns one of the hills of the Island. This tower was built about the time of the Union, and it survived practically unimpaired while the Union itself remained. Then, only a few years ago, a late watcher in a night of storm saw a sudden fire fall from Heaven; and boys going out in the morning to visit their rabbit-snares brought back the news that the tower had been split in sunder by a thunderbolt in the night. Its day was out and its ruin accomplished.

During its life of a century legends had begun to accumulate about it, and the people of middle age tell one how the old women were accustomed to terrify them in their childhood with tales of the White Lady of the Tower, a vague spectral apparition of which nothing definite remains to be gathered now. Another tale of the tower has more of the authentic colour of history. I heard it first from a man herding a cow on the slope of the hill farther back along the Island beyond the Tower. It was a warm day in autumn, and I had wandered along the road to where it ends in a broad space of less abrupt declivity than the rest of the hill-slope, still named An Pháirc, the field, and showing yet in the marks of old ridges and in its place-names the traces of ancient cultivation. It is said that as many as seven plough-teams have been seen at work here, all hidden from one another by the rolling of the irregular surface. But it is too far from the houses to be worked now, and cows and sheep alone wander over it, cropping the sweet grass which grows the richer for that abandoned tillage.

I was drowsy with the sun and the blue glitter of the sea, and, finding a convenient turf-rick, lay down in its shelter and dreamed indolently over my book. In those solitary spaces an irresistible magnetism draws human beings together, and before long a shadow fell across me, and looking up I saw that the herd had left his cow and had come across in the hope of finding a more talkative companion. He leaned over me and spoke.

'The eye is not sated with seeing nor is the ear filled with hearing.'

'That is a strange saying,' I said. 'Where did you get it?'

'You would say it was a proverb,' he replied, 'but it was from a book I got it.'

'And what book was that?'

'It was the book the wise man whose name was Thomas à Kempis wrote in Latin centuries ago.'

'And did you read it in Latin?'

'No, I didn't read it at all. But the Latin book was turned into Irish by a man of my name, one of the O'Sullivans, and a minister on the mainland had the book, and he lent it to a man on the Island, one of the Soupers, who could read. I heard him reading the book when I was young, and I have that saying ever since.'

'Well,' I said, 'it is strange how things happen. I have seen that saying printed in a book of the proverbs of the Irish, and yet it comes from Thomas à Kempis, and even he didn't say it first, for it is from the Bible itself that he had it.'

'I don't find that strange,' he said, 'for even the proverbs had their beginning; some man said every proverb out of his own mind at the first, and why wouldn't one of them come from the Bible itself?'

'You are right,' I answered, and we let the question of the origin of proverbs drift from us, for it was too hot to be bothering the mind with the why and the wherefore of things. He lit a pipe and I a cigarette, and we watched the smoke drifting up into the moveless air, the one or the other of us letting drop a listless word now and then as the humour took us. The intermitted talk wandered as idly as the smoke from one thing to another, till at last it settled on the Tower, which a fold of the hill behind us hid from our view.

'Did you ever hear,' he asked, 'of the French ship that fired a cannon-ball at the Island?'

'I did not,' I answered. 'Why would it be firing at the Island?'

'It was this way it fell out. There was a man of the Island talking with two of the soldiers of the Tower up there on the ridge of the hill, and they looked out to sea, and what should they see but a ship sailing towards the Island. "That's a ship of war," said one of the soldiers, "and what's more it's a French ship."

'They were looking thus when a white smoke came out of the side of the ship. The soldiers knew well what it was, and they fell down on their faces on the ground. But the poor fool of an islander had never seen its like before, and he remained standing upright till he heard a great noise from the ship, and a ball came flying over him and buried itself in the ground beyond where they were. It's then he understood what it was, and I promise you it wasn't long till he joined the soldiers on the ground with the fear of death in his heart.'

This solitary shot is all of war that the Tower ever saw,

and until the bolt from Heaven, better directed than the French cannon-ball, shattered its walls, it stood unbroken on its hill. After the wars a few soldiers were left to guard it; then these were withdrawn, and a single watchman had charge of it—Maurice of the Tower, he was called—and at last, in the Island phrase, the King had no further use for Maurice himself, and the White Lady moved in, to be herself dislodged, one supposes, by the flame from the skies.

Seán Ó Duínnlé, though he lived to be an old man, had a shorter life than his coeval tower. He was not born on the Island, but came in, as did most of the ancestors of the present inhabitants, from the mainland. Of his early life before he commenced poet nothing is recorded. It was in the years of the Great Famine that the vein of poetry first pulsed in him, and the story goes that indignation made him a poet. He was a great *spailpín*, a wandering harvester, who in the season would sling his reaping-hook over his shoulder and go *síos amach*, northwards into Kerry and Cork and even to County Limerick. On these wanderings he acquired an immense store of knowledge, tales and poems and sayings, all that vast flood of popular tradition which remained while Irish was still a living power, and of which we painfully collect the flotsam on the ebb to-day. In Ireland, as in medieval Europe, the tales spread among the people of the roads, the wandering harvesters, the tramping men and the beggars, the poor scholars and poets and migratory schoolmasters. Seán had graduated in this university of the road; and if we find, as I have found on the Island, a tale which can be traced back, through the jest-books of the Middle Ages and the sermon-books of the preaching friars to the Arabs of Africa, and through Persian books to ancient India, it is by such men that it has been carried from extremest East to farthest West, to die at last by a turf fire within hearing of the Atlantic wave.

He came back from one of his pilgrimages with money in his pocket, and, going into the Dingle sheep-market on his way through, saw a fine sheep that he fancied there. He had no sheep at home, and he thought that this would make a fine beginning for a flock. So he bought it, conveyed it to Dunquin, tied its legs together, and threw it into a boat which carried them both home to the Island. There he set it free on the hill, and settled down in his house, at the top of the village where now is only a bare space with no vestige of a human dwelling, and took his ease after his wanderings, dreaming of the fine flock that was to grow out of this single sheep. But he reckoned without his neighbours. There were some evil characters in the village, and before long news came to him that the sheep was killed and eaten. Anger came upon him, to think of the wicked folk who had eaten his dream of prosperity, and he swore he would have the law of them at the court of Tralee.

There was another case pending over the unfortunate islanders. In those days the Tiaracht was owned by a rich lady of the Dingle neighbourhood named Betty Rice. The puffins used to come from overseas at the beginning of spring to nest in that solitary pyramid of the sea, and, when their young had come to a certain stage in their growth, they were fine fat birds, the best eating in the world, and the best kitchen to potatoes that the heart could desire. Betty Rice used to send a boat to the Island at this season to kill the young of the puffins—*fuipíní* they were called—for the servants on her farm to eat. The islanders held that there was no property in the birds of the air; and, acting on this excellent theory, they were wont to anticipate Betty's boat and kill the *fuipíní* for themselves, for their potatoes were dry eating without something to take the monotony off them. In the year of Seán's misfortune, a boat had set out and spent a great

day among the birds; but when they were coming back
to the harbour in the evening, who should they see on
shore but Betty's steward, who had come to muster a
boat's crew for the morrow's expedition. They were
caught red-handed; the steward went home in a passion
and told his mistress that there would be nothing for her
servants that year, for the islanders had made a ruin of the
rock and had left nothing behind them. She was fit to be
tied with rage, and swore that they should go to prison for
their robbery.

The time of the court came, and half the Island set out
for Tralee, some of them to argue the case with Betty Rice,
and others to meet the charge of the stolen sheep. Betty's
prisoners went to friends in Dingle, who appealed to her
mercy, but she would not listen to them, and by her
manner so angered them that they swore they would do
their best to procure the failure of her cause. They went
to Tralee with the islanders and spoke overnight to Daniel
O'Connell.

On the next day, when the court was opened, the
Counsellor, as the people called him, was there, sitting
half asleep while Betty's man of law detailed the wrong
that had been done to her and her servants. When he had
finished, the Counsellor woke up and craved the hearing
of the court. It was a case of something near to starvation,
he said; the islanders had never done such a thing before,
and would never do it again, but sheer need and the
monotony of their potato diet had so afflicted them and
their children that they had to go after the birds; but if
they were let free this time the court might be assured
that it would be long enough before they would set foot
on that fatal rock again.

The eloquence of the great advocate prevailed on the
court, and the islanders were liberated with a warning.
Betty flung out of the court in a rage, and in her disgust

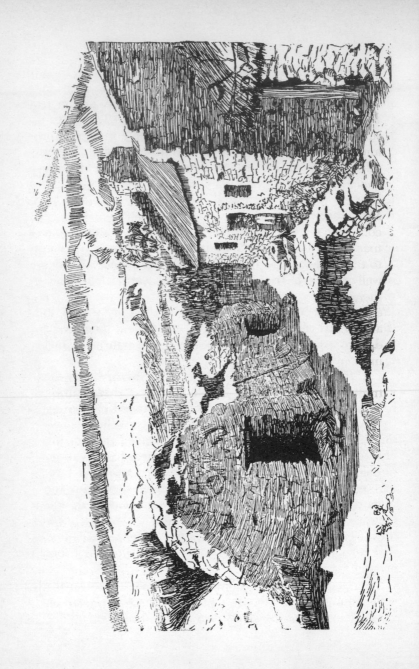

never sent for the birds again, so that they were free game ever after.

Seán's case now came on, and, when his complaint had been made, the great Counsellor, exhilarated by his success, broke in again, arguing that it was a trivial matter, and if Seán had the price of his sheep and his costs he ought to be satisfied. The court agreed, and the angry *spailpín* had to forgo his hope that the thieves would pay by a term of prison for the wrong they had done him. He went home as furious as Betty herself, and fell to the composition of a venomous satire, the first poem he ever made, and a bitter one it was. It would be vain to attempt to translate into English that litany of curses, but we may well believe that the thieves would gladly have served their term of prison if the weight of that commination could have been lifted from their shoulders. This just anger had unlocked the poet's lips, and till the day of his death he never failed to celebrate every notable occasion in fluent verse.

His poetry is the poetry of the countryside, full of traditional idiom and the lively turns of speech born of the sharpening of wit upon wit in the banter of every day. Its subjects are the tragedies and humours and triumphs of the simple village life. A sudden storm overwhelms a boat in Ventry Bay, a woman of the Island weaves herself a quilt, the poet's ass dies, an Island boat wins a race, a cartful of people coming home well primed from market is overset by the roadside, a farmer is evicted in the Land War, an old man marries a young wife—these and a dozen other happenings become the talk of the country-side, and the poet is on hand with his verses, which are passed delightedly from mouth to mouth, every stroke going home among a people nursed in such poetry, and electrically alive to each turn of phrase, each trait of character, each subtilty of allusion to events known to everybody. Taken out of its language and environment, such poetry is like the sea anemone, which lies dead and exhausted on the rocks at the ebb of the tide, but flowers into strange and lively colour when the water of its own element flows over it once more. It can only be read in its own Irish, and can hardly be understood out of its own country-side. Translated and imprisoned in a book the virtue goes out of it, and it becomes a curiosity and a riddle.

Whatever the value of his poetry, Seán got no reward for it but the applause of his fellows. He lived poor and died poor, and it is said was hard put to it to get a drink of milk on his death-bed. There were few cows on the Island in those days, and the poet had no means of procuring milk except by the occasional kindness of a neighbour. There is a verse which he is said to have made on his death-bed, which runs something like this:

> Of all miseries told 'tis the worst to grow old;
> Men leave you to lie like a log;
> Be my thirst what it may, no drink comes my way
> But the slimy black draught from the bog.

And with that he made confession of his sins and died. And with him there went a vast store of now irrecoverable tradition. It is a constant theme with Tomás that we have come too late and that Seán died too early. 'If only the things he had to tell could have been written down,' he says, 'you would have seen something. For he never forgot anything that he had heard once, and he had travelled the world listening, and there was no song or story or saying that he didn't keep in his memory till the day he died. You would listen to him talking all night, and he would never say the same thing twice in the one night. There are no tales in the Island since he died.'

Poets

SHE sat there, the strong woman,
Dark, with swift eyes alert and laughter-lighted,
And gathering that wild flock,
This on her knee, that at her side, another
Crouched hiding elfin-eyed under tossed hair:
A calf, unsteady-footed
And muzzled with a stocking, snuffed and blundered,
And chickens hither and thither
Pecked on the floor, fluttered on loft and settle.
'Poets? And is it Poets?'
She said. 'The day has been when there were poets
Here on the Island, yonder on the mainland.
And my own father's father
Was the chief poet of the Island. Wisha!
You'd go to the well up there to draw the water
And talk a spell maybe, and come back to him
And he'd have the poem for you, clean and clever.
He had the wit. If only he'd had learning,
Mother of God! 'tis he would have been a poet.'

THE POOR SCHOLARS

With Seán Ó Duínnlé, and with others of his kind and generation, passed the latest examples of a type of poet with whom the whole of Europe had an uneasy familiarity throughout the Middle Ages—the goliards, the vagantes, the wandering scholars, by whatever name they were known—essentially the same for many centuries. A Russian scholar has claimed recently that the first goliards of whom we have any real knowledge were the wandering Irish scholars and clerics who were familiar figures upon the roads of Europe before and during the Carolingian time. Besides the great men—a Columbanus, a Gallus, a Fursa, a Johannes Scotus—there swarmed a crowd of forgotten wanderers from court to court, from monastery to monastery, descending on Europe in droves, as a contemporary writer phrases it, putting up learning for sale in the markets, and often vexing the souls of bishops with strange heresies and doctrines unknown to the Councils of the Church. Among such men, living the goliardic life, the characteristic goliardic note began to creep into the formal elegiac verses of the schools.

Before the laughing and lyrical measures of the medieval goliards, Sedulius Scottus—the most typical figure among these peripatetic scholars whose work is accessible to our knowledge—had slipped into the formal parade of Carolingian verse the themes and phrases which were to go upon a lighter foot in a later time. And one would need to be at little trouble to collect instances up and down Irish literature of the light, reckless, impudent topical verses which everywhere mark the emergence of this type. Those who know the tale of Mac Conglinne will recognize at once in this scholar, who leaves the shade of his studies and takes to poetry and the wandering life, the perfect image of a goliard, and in his story, with its strange blend of ironic pedantry, mocking theology, and transformed folk themes, the most fascinating of the goliardic creations, until the kind finds its apotheosis in the life and poetry of François Villon, and the confused and wonderful epic of Rabelais.

In Ireland, where the ruin of the seventeenth century scattered the students of the schools and the followers of their tradition among the common folk, the wandering scholar—schoolmaster, poet, and musician—was a known figure wherever anything of the old life survived until only the other day. And their influence and their tradition is responsible for most of the modern literature in Irish. In the people's memory two figures of this kind stand out distinct—the witty, inspired, improvising poet, and the poor scholar travelling from house to house with his bag of books, solving knotty problems with the aid of his recondite learning, and often by a parade of scholarship getting the upper hand among a people unlearned, but passionate admirers of printed knowledge and strange tongues. A tale I heard on the Island will show how a poor scholar of this kind could be trusted to fathom a mystery of the most insoluble order. It was told to me by Peig to explain the name 'Caisleán an Mhúraigh', 'Moore's Castle', which had come up in desultory talk.

'Moore was a rich man who lived in the old times over yonder to the north, and he built a fine castle by the sea. And when he had the castle built, he said to himself that it was a great shame that he had no heir to leave the castle to when he came to die. So he sought a woman for his wife, one of the loveliest women of her time, and they were married and lived together for thirteen years, but in all that time they had no child, boy or girl, and Moore thought that he would die with no heir to leave the

castle to   But one day in the summer Moore's wife said
to herself that she would go swimming in the sea. So she
went down to the strand—a fine white shore of sand it
was—and took her clothes off her and swam out into
the sea. She had gone some way out in the bay when
she looked down beneath her, and what should she see
floating in the water below her feet but the shadow of a
man. Fear came on her then and she turned and swam
towards the land. But as she swam the shadow followed,
and when she swam slowly the shadow went slowly too,
and when she hastened it hastened in the water under her.

'They were going thus ever and always till she came to
land, and she walked trembling up the shore to where she
had left her clothes and fell fainting on them. When she
came to herself again there was no one there but herself
alone, and she put on her clothes and went back to the
castle with the fear still heavy on her. When the time was
come she bore a child, the loveliest of children ever seen
in those parts, and as the child grew all men marvelled
at him, and loved him for his beauty and gentleness, and
the one way he had with high and low. But there was a
strange thing about him, that never from the day he was
born did he as much as close an eye to sleep. He would
see all about him when the night came lying down and
closing their eyes and staying there without moving until
the day whitened over them in the morning. But he never
slept, nor once felt the need of sleep. This was a great
wonder to him, but he could never make out for himself,
nor could anyone tell him, why this want of sleep had
come upon him.

'One day in the late evening there came a poor scholar
to the castle with his bag of books, and asked would they
give him a meal and leave to be inside from the air of the
night. They said they would and welcome. So he came
in, and when he had eaten he sat down by the fire with

Moore's son, and they stayed there talking when all the others had gone to bed. At last the scholar rose up from his corner, and "Wisha," said he, "it is getting late, and I am tired from long walking on little food, and maybe it would be as well for me to be going to sleep." "It would," said Moore's son. "Good night to you." "And won't you be going to sleep yourself?" said the poor scholar. "I will not," said he, "for from the day I was born I have never known what sleep is." "Do you tell me that?" said the poor scholar. "I do," said he. "And I never knew, nor could any tell me, why this was, or of what people I am. But you that have walked the world and have read many books, perhaps you might have the knowledge of a people in some part of the world that never sleep?" "Maybe I might," said he, "for I remember to have read in a book of such a people, and, by the same token, I have that same book in my bag." And he opened his bag and was searching in it until at the very bottom of the bag he found a little old torn book, and in the very end of the book he found the story he looked for.

' "I have it here," he said. "He says in this book that there is a people in the world that never sleep, and it is in the sea that people has its dwelling." "Then," said Moore's son, "it is of the people of the sea I am." And he took a sword down from the wall, and he went into his mother's room, and held the sword over the bed. She woke up and saw the shining of the sword above her. "What do you want of me, my son?" said she, "that you hold the sword over my head?" "It is the story of my birth I want, and what happened you before it," he said. "You are very hard on me, my son," she said, "but since you ask it of me and the sword in your hand I will tell you." And she told him the whole story from beginning to end. "Then," he said, "the poor scholar had the truth of it, and it is of the people of the sea I am."

'On the next day he gathered together all his friends, and he went down to the brink of the sea and stood there. And it wasn't long till they saw a great wave far out in the sea, and it came in to land, and they saw a man in the wave, the most beautiful any of them had ever seen. And the lad bade farewell to his friends and went down into the sea. The wave came up round him and the man in it, and the man cast his arms about the lad, and the wave went back into the sea and they with it. And from that day to this no one has ever seen sign or token of Moore's son.'

Nobody but a wandering scholar could have solved that problem, or given the answer to many another question of like or greater difficulty put to them in the lonely town-lands to which they brought the rumour of a wider world. They are gone now, and the fashion of the life they knew has gone with them. The people read newspapers, and in the police barracks at Ballyferriter near Moore's Castle a wireless set strikes wonder into the country people. 'Yes,' said one of the islanders to me the other day, 'I sat in the barracks and I saw a man dancing a hornpipe, and a fiddler in London was playing the music for that dance. It is the greatest marvel ever I saw.'

This is a riddle beyond the wit of the wandering scholars, but perhaps they had a secret of the light foot and the merry heart which is ill exchanged for a music that leaps sea and land to be trapped at last in a machine.

GOING WEST

I WOKE one morning of spring long before there was any stir in the house or in the village without. My bed was at one end of the room away from the window, a solid structure of four posts built up against the outer wall, floored with boards stretched across the frame, their hardness alleviated by a mattress stuffed with the feathers of seabirds. This mattress is beautifully soft when you go to bed at night, but by morning your weight has worked through the feathers, and the hardness of the boards begins to make itself felt. I got up and shook the feathers up a little, and then went over to the window and took down the blind. Beyond the quiet village I could see a strip of water and the head of Dún Mór thrusting out into the Sound. The day was heavy with cloud, and there was nothing in the morning to invite one into the air from a warm bed. So I took a book and went back to the birds' feathers. The book was the poems of Eoghan Ruadh Ó Súilleabháin, and drowsily I crooned over to myself those lines of complicated melody, filled with rich words whose chiming syllables echo to one another down the long stanzas.

There is something hypnotic in those cloying melodies, and I had dropped back into a half-sleep when I was suddenly startled into broad waking. A man shouted outside, there was a scuffle and a rush, and with a tremendous impact something struck the roof above my head, struggled there for a moment, found its feet and scuffled off again with a clatter of hurrying hoofs. I had looked to see it come through the felt and timber of the roof, and then I might have known what creature had fallen out of the sky above my head.

But the roof held, and I was left alone with the mystery.

Soon there was a stirring in the kitchen. My hostess, Máire, the King's daughter, was up and busy about the fire. I dressed and went out, and after the morning greeting told my story.

'I don't know what it can have been,' said she, 'but it's a mercy it didn't come through on your head.'

'I wouldn't have much to boast about if it had,' I answered, 'for there was a great weight in it.' Then I pulled open the half-door and went out.

The house, like most of the houses of the older fashion, is built into a high bank for shelter, and at the end the bank rises above the level of the roof. A path runs along this bank and past the back of the house, and just beyond the path is a walled garden of cabbage-plants. This was the solution of the mystery. The pasturage on the hill for sheep is poor and thin, and, if a ewe has two lambs in the spring, she has not milk enough to rear them both, so it is the custom to bring one of them back to the house and rear it by hand. Such home-bred lambs are known as 'Betties', and, being given the run of the house, and fed on milk and bread and potatoes, they grow strong and fearless and impudent, and develop a thievish habit of taking their food where they find it. One such Betty, in its second year, strolling along the path in the deserted morning, had leapt the wall of the cabbage-garden, and had been discovered filling its belly with the green leaves. The owner of the garden had jabbed at it with a potato-spade, and the terrified Betty, leaping the wall again, had been carried over the path with the impetus of that leap, and had fallen with a noise of thunder on the roof above my head. It was long before I heard the last of this morning fright.

An hour later I was finishing my breakfast at the table by the window, on the outer sill of which a hen perched with ruffled feathers, looking in on me through the glass with the blank, incurious eye of her kind, when a great figure darkened the doorway, and Seán an Rígh, the King's son, came in.

'We are going to Inisicíleáin to hunt rabbits,' he said. 'Will you come with us, Bláheen?'

I had long wanted to explore the Inis, and I left my breakfast and the hen, fetched my coat, and went down to the harbour with Seán. Another of the fishermen and two lads and an eager company of dogs were waiting there. We dived under the naomhóg where it rested on its strut, heaved it on to our shoulders, and picked our way down the treacherous slip, slimy at the foot with weed and the deposit of the sea. Tipping the boat from our shoulders, we slipped it into the water, and, barking and shouldering one another, the excited dogs tumbled into it. The men put aboard the sail and the oars and a spade or two, the last on land thrust her into the sea, a wanton flick of the water washing over his boots as he did so, and we were gliding out through the mouth of the harbour under the indifferent gaze of a little group of children perched on the cliff.

We turned An Gob, the beak of the Island, and, keeping close inshore, followed the line of the cliffs westward over the restless sea. For though the heavy clouds hung without visible movement in the calm sky, the water remembered a week of wind, and the waves were running into broken white crests which flickered here and there on a dull field of sea grey under a grey heaven. The cliffs inshore showed black where water and wind had weathered the surface of the old red sandstone, with here and there a glint of livelier colour as the sea washed over their bases and fell back defeated.

Where the scant grass began above the confusion of rocks, sheep were feeding unconcernedly above the abyss, the new lambs looking incredibly fragile and awkward on their stiff legs. Some had even ventured out on the cliffs, hunting the sweet grass that springs in the crannies of the rocks. There are places in the cliffs that the islanders call *draipeanna*, little islands of good grass among the bare rocks; and now and again a sheep or a cow or an ass, more venturesome than its fellows, follows the lure of this uncropped pasture, and finds itself trapped there when it thinks of returning as it came, and then the owner must go down the precipitous cliff with a rope, and with the help of his fellows recover his strayed beast. The men in their prime are expert cliffsmen, and it is terrifying to see them running over the sheer cliff in places where you would say that a goat could find no foothold. But even they are caught at times in such places, and must be taken out with a rope.

Tomás has a tale of a climber who was trapped so in the time of the Great Famine, when, he says, 'They were close run for food, for when the produce of the year should have come up, there was nothing in the earth, and so they had to betake themselves to the strand or the hill or any place where they could take bird or fish. There was a man in the Island in those days whose nickname was Púdar, and no bird ever laid an egg in a place where Púdar wouldn't take both egg and bird. If there was any place where he couldn't go, neither could a cat go there. One day that he was out fishing with a seine net, there was no fish in the sea, and they turned home early, and they saw at the western end of the Island, high up in the cliff, a great company of fine fat birds, each bird with an egg laid; and birds of this kind, puffin, guillemot, and the like, never lay but the one egg. A place like this is called a *sgairt*, a great hole running up into it with a wide opening at the mouth. "If you could put me ashore," says Púdar, "I would climb up, and the boat wouldn't be going home so empty as she is." "Sure, you wouldn't be able to

go where those birds are even if you were ashore," says
the captain of the boat. "Och, I'd go easily enough if
I were on land," says he.

'They had to land him, though they had no hope of a
bird, and never looked to see him back again, for they had
to shut their eyes when they saw him going up through the
cliff. Very soon he reached the mouth of the *sgairt*, drove
the birds back into the hole, and fell to throttling them and
throwing them down on the sea to the boat, till he had ten
dozen of them floating and the boat picking them up.
When he had the last of them killed and thrown down,
the captain called up to him, "What's keeping you up
there?" he said. "You'd best be starting down so that we
can be going home, for the day is getting late." The man
on the cliff spoke and said: "I can never go down, and I'm
sure I can't go up either, for if a rope were sent down to
me it would be forty feet out from me. Home with you in
God's name," said Púdar, "for I think those are the last
birds I shall ever kill," said he.

'The boat started home with one of the crew lacking,
and if they had been proud before of all the birds they had
in the boat, they had little to say now, for the man that
had sent the birds down to them was gone. A sad, sorrowful night it was among the neighbours, to say nothing of
his own people.

'When the day broke, all the people in the place went
up the hill with ropes, but when they came in sight of the
sgairt he was standing in the mouth of the hole, and when
they came to the place where he was there was no chance
at all of taking him out of it; if a rope were to be lowered
in his direction it would go out over the sea.

'A son of Púdar's not twenty years of age was among the
men. "Lower me down on a big rope," he said, "and I'll
take a coil of thin rope to him, he's not a lost man yet."
"But perhaps you will go dizzy," said one of the men.

"No fear of that," said he. They lowered him down till he was level with his father. He knotted the cord round the big rope and coiled up the rest of it. Then he told his father to move out into the brink as far as he could, and to stretch out his arm as far as he could.

'The father did so, you may be sure. Then the lad aimed the coil at his father and cast it towards the mouth of the *sgairt*, and it went over his father's arm at that cast. "Good luck," said his father, "you'll do it yet." "Draw the big rope in to you," said the son, "until you have your hand round it, and don't let it go too easily." And he stayed down there hanging till his father had the rope in his fist. Then the son made his way up with his hands and feet like a cat till he reached the top. They all shook hands with him as heartily as though he had been a year and twenty in the States, and it wasn't long till they had Púdar himself with them on the level ground, and anybody there would have thought that he was Oisín returned from Tír na nÓg.

'For all his life after Púdar was always careful to scan a cliff narrowly before ever he went into it. His son too was no "craftsman's son that grew into a blunderer"; he went to sea and afterwards became a good sailor.'

Talking of this and other scapes on the cliff we had come far back along the Island, the men as they rowed always on the look-out for sheep and rabbits, and mocking at the tiny men and women and children that moved like flies along the high lift of the hill.

We came at last to Ceann Dubh, the Black Head, at the Island's end, and passed out into the space of water, An Bealach Mór, the Great Channel, which separates the Great Blasket from its smaller fellows. The channel goes out into the open sea, and here we felt at once the lift of the long Atlantic swell that came rolling in, carrying the little broken waves on its back. Before us was Inis na Bró, Quern Island, so called because some fanciful eye once saw a resemblance in it to the handmills with which grain used to be ground. At the end of Inis na Bró the cliff goes up in a series of gradations known as Steipeacha an Amadáin Mhóir, 'the steps of the Great Fool', no doubt because it was anciently fabled that that odd figure of Irish story went up them once with what the old romances call 'a light swift birdlike leap'.

We drew in to the side of the island to land the boys with their spades and dogs. The dogs had gone into the bows and whined and barked as the boat drew near to the rocks; then at an oar's length they leapt ashore. The two men held the boat's prow to the rock with deft strokes of the oar, and as she came up on the wave the boys, one after another, sprang lightly ashore. Their spades were flung after them, and we made for Inisicílcáin.

'Were there ever any people living on Inis na Bró?' I asked Seán an Rígh.

'Not that I know,' was the answer, 'but there is a *múchán* (an old stone house) there, and hunters spend the night there sometimes. The old people have a tale that once there were three men caught by a storm on the island. They made a fire of seapink and sat round it talking. In the middle of the night they heard a noise on the roof like men fighting, and it went on so for a long time without ceasing. "I'll go out to see what it is," said one of them. "Don't go," said the others, "for fear it might be some evil thing, for there are no living beings on the island only ourselves." But the fighting went on more and more, and at last, for all they could say, he went out.

'And when he had gone out, the noise was louder for a time, and it went down off the roof, and they heard it going from them across the island, and at last it was so far from them that they thought it was as far as the brink of the cliff, and then it stopped suddenly, and all that night they heard nothing more. And when the day was come they went out, and walked the whole island, but they found no trace of the man who had gone out, and from that day to this he has never been seen again.'

'What was it that had taken him?' I asked.

'Nobody knows. Some say it was the fairies or some evil thing, but there were those that said that the two men had killed the other man and had made up the tale between them.'

INISICILEAIN

WE had now come to the landing on Inisicíleáin, and with sedulous care, for the beach is open and exposed, and the breaking waves were making a yeasty turmoil at the edge of the tide, they brought the boat in to shore. Our dogs were out in a moment, and we not far behind them. When the boat was safely stowed under the cliff, we climbed the winding path that leads dangerously to the summit. Off ran the dogs, snuffing and burrowing in the crumbling soil along the cliff edge. Soon it was plain that they were on a hot scent, and the men fell to digging out the hole till they came on a hapless rabbit crouching terrified in the last cover. A twist of the hand finished him, and the dogs were away to another hole.

I soon grew weary of this monotonous sport, and drifted away over the island out of sound of the slaughter. For some way from the landing-place it is a flat table-land above the sea, but soon the land begins to rise, and at last a great wall of towering rocks shuts off the far end of the island. Approaching this wall from the level ground you have the feeling that it hides a secret; there is something so definite and planned about it, as though some giant creatures surviving out of the world before man had here been minded to make their last refuge. For the whole island is inhabited with the sense of loneliness; it is as though it were at the last end of things, dwelling in a silence which the ceaseless murmur of the sea round its base and the whining gulls about its summit rather accentuate than disturb. It is perhaps this feeling which comes upon one involuntarily as one wanders alone through that silence which has made it in the people's minds the chosen haunt of the fairies. 'Are there any fairies in the Inis?' they will say. 'Why, it is black with them!' And if ever things invisible ventured over the dividing threshold of the two worlds, it is here one feels that they would choose to put on a frail body in mimicry of mortality, and dance on the grassy floors above the cliff under the moon.

In the old days, when this island was inhabited, a man sat alone one night in his house, soothing his loneliness with a fiddle. He was playing, no doubt, the favourite music of the country-side, jigs and reels and hornpipes, the hurrying tunes that would put light heels on the feet of the dead. But, as he played, he heard another music without, going over the roof in the air. It passed away to the cliffs and returned again, and so backwards and forwards again and again, a wandering air wailing in repeated phrases, till at last it had become familiar in his mind, and he took up the fallen bow, and drawing it across the strings followed note by note the lamenting voices as they passed above him. Ever since, that tune, *port na bpúcaí*, 'the fairy music', has remained with his family, skilled musicians all, and, if you hear it played by a fiddler of that race, you will know the secret of Inisicíleáin. The fairies, they say, are not immortal, they, too, know death, and the music that went over the house on the island that night was a lament for one of the fairy host that had died and was carried to this island for burial. How easily could one believe that, beyond this vast wall, the whole fairy race that once were dreams more real than living men had fled for sepulture, when the cold truths of reason had glared upon their fragility, and driven them even from the light of the moon. That fairy music, played upon an island fiddle, is a lament for a whole world of imaginations banished irrevocably now, but still faintly visible in the afterglow of a sunken sun.

I climbed the wall now, scrambling on hands and knees, and came into the place it guarded. Here was a huge confusion of rock pillars, leaning every way, supporting one another or mounted upon one another, and suggesting in their wild architecture the ruin of some mighty temple, the building of which had been interrupted by a natural calamity overwhelming temple and builders in one common ruin. I clambered to the summit of the highest pillar, and sat down in a crevice on its side. From this high tower an immense prospect was disclosed, the islands and the Atlantic on the left side, and on the right Dingle Bay, between its two enclosing peninsulas of Corca Dhuibhne and Íbh Ráthach. The day was still muffled in cloud, but an opalescent light trembling in that grey roof, and a brightness falling through crevices here and there at random on sea or hill showed that the sun was shining in the clear air above the clouds. Heavy vapours hung condensed on the mountain summits, and along the sides of the hills a lazy smoke dallied and trailed for lack of wind to carry it away. It was the turf-cutting season, and they were firing the furze to lighten the work of stripping the hill. The mountains at the head of Dingle Bay were lost in a liquid haze, milky blue in colour, the hue of a clouded pearl.

From that invisible distance the range of hills of Íbh Ráthach stretched under the unchanging pall of cloud, ending at last in Valencia Island, and, far from the last point of land, the two abrupt islands of the Skelligs stood out into the sea like two great ships in full sail for the undiscovered west. As I looked, the wandering sunrays came to rest for a moment on the summit of the Great Skellig, and something flashed there a moment and was gone.

There is an old church on Inisicíleáin, and this island, too, was once a dwelling of the religious. The old manuscripts tell us nothing of these settlements, and it is only in a fourteenth-century chronicle of Ratisbon that the legend of the early days of the Great Skellig is to be found. Here it was, says the story, that St. Patrick drove the evil things and venomous serpents out of Ireland into the Western Sea. The saint is often compared to Moses in the old writings, and he imitated Moses in this, too, for it was by holding his arms aloft in prayer, like Moses in the battle with the Amalekites, that he routed the devils and the poisonous creatures. For when he raised his arms, says the manuscript, 'the tempests fell silent, the winds were laid, the rains were at peace, the air shone clear, the fear of the holy ones was allayed, the night grew bright as day, and all the coasts of Ireland took light from the hands of the saint that were as the sun glittering with the radiance of noonday.

'And lifting up their eyes in this light, the holy ones beheld St. Michael, with many cohorts of angels gathered about him, standing in a certain place withdrawn into the farthest ocean, where is a certain crag surrounded on every side by the eddies of the great sea. At the which vision they fell all to the ground and besought him of his favour to come to their aid, and, forasmuch as in the sight of God and His angels the cry of the holy ones cannot be of no avail, St. Michael came in his might, his splendid company all glittering about him. And at his coming the holy ones renewed and resumed their strength, and climbed the mount, whither a way was prepared for them by the hands of the angels through the constructions wherewith the devils had girt the mountain round about, and this way is called the Path of the Saints until this day.

'And every one of the saints, smiting with a sword and making the sign of the holy cross against the opposing host, so ascended to the summit of the mountain. The foe were confounded and their might shattered, and they turned their backs to the holy ones, and, rushing all together, the venomous creatures and the devils alike were flung into the gulf of the vast ocean, the saints and the angels alike lending aid to one another. And, this accomplished, Saint Michael the Archangel with all his company returned to the crag whence he had come to the aid of the holy ones, and, ascending thence into heaven, left behind him a shield which heals all diseases and wounds, nor can any man ascertain of what substance it is, whether of wood, stone, iron, or bronze, neither can any earthly craft boast for itself the making of such a shield.

'And so this habitation has been assigned by heaven to holy men desiring to lead a solitary life. For that crag is distant a day's sail from the land with a favouring wind. And in such manner doth the ocean rave about it that no ship of wood can sustain without destruction the clash of the waves, nor can men go or come from Ireland in the said island at any season of the year save between the feasts of St. Philip and St. James and the feast of St. Michael, and that in vessels made of hides and smeared with the most tenacious pitch.'

So in medieval Latin the German chronicler, peering dimly through wide spaces of time and distance, tells the tale.

Was it, perhaps, the shield of Michael Archangel that flashed out a signal from the summit of the rock as I stood at gaze that day, on the very spot from which the hermits of Inisicíleáin must often have looked across the water towards their fellows of the Skellig? But in a moment the light had left the crag, and was running out into the ocean like the light of St. Patrick's uplifted hands following the devils to their last retreats.

There is an old story of the origin of the fairies, that when St. Michael and his hosts cast Lucifer and his insurgent angels over the wall of Heaven, they fell head-long into Hell, and the lid of Hell was made fast over them, but at the closing of Hell some were still falling through the air; and these, finding no home, whether with the good or evil angels, remained suspended in the air, and these are the fairies. So, too, one might imagine that some of the devils driven westwards from the Skelligs had taken refuge on Inisicíleáin among these great rocks, 'the construction of the devils', and that the fairies of the Inis are of their kin. The problem may be left to those learned in demonology and fairy lore. But there is certainly no place more fitted for the last home of the 'angels of pride' than this broken end of Inisicíleáin.

I went on now to complete the circuit of the cliffs. Coming out on the side that looks towards the flank of the Great Blasket, a weariness fell on me, and I threw myself down on the grass at the edge of a steep descent. Half-way to the sea below me a grassy ledge stood out from the face of the cliff, and, looking down on this ledge, I saw some four or five rabbits leap out of their holes and begin to play. It was the breeding season, and there were tiny creatures among them, hardly more than a hand's length in size. These little ones chased one another up and down the ledge, while at first the larger ones looked on. Then these, too, caught the infection and began to play. One of them would lie down on the grass while another leaped backwards and forwards across him. Then they would run at one another in a mimic fight, and roll over on the grass struggling. Then the whole company would race wildly up and down the green ledge, bucking into the air at intervals. It was strange to see them sporting unconsciously, as though in some Eden before the coming of man on the earth, while on the other side of the island men were slaughtering their fellows. Before long a cramp came in my leg as I lay and I moved slightly, and in that moment the ledge was empty once more. Man had come into the world, and the wild creatures fled from their ruined Eden.

I heard now a faint calling on the air, and made my way

in the direction of the sound. The others had finished
their business and were standing by the house of the island,
the rabbits hanging from spades on their shoulders with
limp bodies and pitifully beblooded noses. The bag had
been a small one, hardly worth the trouble of the row.
One of the men had a key, and he opened the door of the
house and we went in. It was a bare, gaunt house, lacking
even the scant luxuries of the Island dwellings. For the
last of the O'Dalys only comes here during the week
throughout the summer, returning to the main Island for
the Sunday. In the old days as many as five or six families
have lived in this island, planting crops and herding sheep
and fishing. The soil is rich, too rich they say for potatoes,
which send up here so luxuriant a leafage that they
exhaust their strength in that effort, and few potatoes come
under the ground. But it is a good earth for cabbages and
onions and the like, and they say that even tobacco has
been grown here.

Little more than a generation ago a strange calamity,
strangely heralded, fell upon the tiny company. There
were three families living on the island at the time, three
men and their women and children. One day a man
wanted to go to Dingle upon some pressing need, but the
other men would not go with him. So he took a small
boat and started by himself to row the length of the bay,
some sixteen miles of sea. When he got clear of Inisicíleáin he glanced over the side of the boat, and there
beside him as he rowed the sea opened, and looking down,
he could see through walls of water to the bottom, and a
road ran along the bottom and three men were walking
on the road. He thought by rowing hard to escape the
fear of that vision, but as he hastened the three men
quickened their pace, and when he rested on his oars they
also rested. So the strange journey went on, the man half-
dead with terror, yet pulling mechanically with the

automatic habit of the sea, and the spectral three going easily and unperturbed along the bottom of the bay.

At last, he scarcely knew how, he came to Dingle, and they had to lift him from the boat, for he could not stand for the fears of that passage. He dared not attempt the way home, but the next day a trawler from Dingle was going fishing round the island, and they carried him and his boat back with them. When he returned, he said nothing of his adventure to the other men, but gave some hint of it to his wife.

A day or two after, the three men went out fishing, and by some misadventure the boat was overset, and all three were drowned. That day, on the great Island, when they went back along the hill to carry turf, they saw the smoke of a fire on Inisicíleáin, and that was an agreed signal when any danger or stress threatened the little isolated community. Men hurried back to the village, a boat set out, and, when they reached the other harbour, they saw the women and children on the cliff above them wailing and half beside themselves with terror. They put out again, and after a long search found the bodies of the three floating on the surface of the water where their prophetic ghosts had walked the road in the depths a few short days before.

'Why did they not take warning from the vision?' I asked Tomás when he told me the tale.

'Dhera,' said he, 'What good would there have been in that? A fisherman must follow the sea, and how can a man escape the day of his death? There is such and such a time marked out for a man on this earth, and, when his day is come, if he went into an ant's hole, death would find him there. We have only our time, and, young or old, a man must go when he is called. There was a boat going out to Inis Tuaisceart once to fish from the rocks, and when they were half-way out they found that they had

left the mast behind them. So they went back for the mast.
And there was a man on the slip who was the best man
on the Island at fishing from the rocks, for at every craft
there is one man is better than all others, if it were only at
driving nails with a hammer. They set out again, taking
this man with them, and, when they came to Inis Tuaisceart, they went about the island putting one man out on
a rock here and another there, till at last they were all in
their places fishing. After they had been thus for a time,
the day began to rise on them, and the boat went again to
pick up the men; but when they came to the rock where
they had put this man out, he was not to be found. A
wave had come up out of the sea, they said, and taken him,
for death wanted him and his day was come, and when
they went back at the beginning of the day it was not for
the mast they went, as they thought, but for the man.
No man goes beyond his day.'

The last to live on the Inis were two of the Dalys, father
and mother of the Daly who still has the house. Their
children left them one by one, and at last they, too, had to
come to the great Island; and at length, the woman first
and then the man, they sickened, and, going to the Work-
house hospital in Dingle, died there out of the sound of
the sea.

THE SEAL

IT was growing late now, and the sun was far down towards the Atlantic horizon, so we climbed down the cliff, ran the boat down through the surf, and crossed the narrow strait to Inis na Bró. The boys had seen us coming and were waiting on the rock, a heavy burden of rabbits hanging over their shoulders, for they had had better luck than our hunters. Boys and dogs and rabbits came aboard, and running up a sail, for the wind had freshened with the coming on of the evening, we started across the Great Channel to the Black Head of the Island.

As we went the sea broke inshore from us, and a seal put up his melancholy, dripping head, gazed at us for a moment, and then slipped noiselessly back into the sea. This end of the Island is the favourite haunt of the seals, and in the old days the people used to hunt them, selling their skins, eating their flesh, and making oil for their dip-candles from their fat.

'I remember,' said Seán, 'how once when we were coming home from lifting the lobster-pots we came upon a seal asleep on the water. We ran the boat alongside of him, and, as we passed him, I leant over the side and got my arms under him and lifted him into the boat. I give you my word that he woke up then, and he flung himself about in the boat biting. We kept clear of him, and it is as well we did, for he got hold of a thwart of the boat, and it wasn't long till he had that thwart bitten through, and if it had been a leg or an arm of one of us he would have bitten through the leg or the arm just as well. I promise you we were glad enough to get him overboard again, and I make no doubt it was long enough before he took a nap on the top of the water again.'

The seal-chase, indeed, was never without its dangers,

for a bull-seal cornered in a cave is a dangerous customer.
There is a cave with a beach inside in Inisicíleáin and this
was a great breeding-place for the seals in the spring.
One curious tale, half humorous, half ghostly, comes to
its tragic conclusion in this very cave among the seals. It
is the tale of Donnchadh Bocht, and this is how Tomás
told it to me:

'A man from the mainland was married in the Great
Blasket a good while ago. When this man was growing up
in Dunquin parish, he was a tall, strong fellow, but none
the less he hadn't the knowledge of his trade as the other
men in the fishing-boats had, and so he found it hard to
pick up a living among them. When he had been living
like this for a while, he sent a message into the Great
Island, for he had heard that there was a young woman
there with just as little sense as himself, and he said to
himself that maybe they could agree together, and perhaps they would get along as well as anyone else. So it was.
They settled the matter between them, and they were
married and began housekeeping in the Great Blasket.

'The fishermen there would not take him in the boats
either, for they would not be able to trust him, perhaps,
when there was something necessary to be done and he
might do something that would lose the boat, so they would
have nothing to do with him. So he had to find another
means of livelihood, and to go fishing from the shore and
the rocks. His fishing tackle was a great long rod, thirty
feet in length, and a line to correspond.

'He went on like this for a time. One day he was fishing
at the point in this fashion, and he saw the Dunquin boats
coming towards him under full sail, for it was their custom
to fish all round the Blasket. One of the boats saw the man
on the point, and they said to one another that it was
Donnchadh, and that it would be a great pity not to go in

and tell him that his sister was dead since yesterday night. So they lowered the sail and rowed up to the rock and told him. The answer he gave the crew of the boat was that they must tell them, when they went home, that he would rather have lost a five-shilling piece than have her die; "and," he added, "the bream are biting at the point." The crew of the boat thought it strange that he didn't feel more than five-shillings'-worth of sorrow at his sister's death, and they left him there. That boat wasn't gone for long when another boat passed the same point, and as they were going by they saw a wave of the sea swelling up, and it passed behind the man on the rock and carried him headlong down into the depths. They stayed awhile to see would he come to the surface, and he came up after a bit with only the leavings of his breath in him. They put him on shore, and they had to send one of their men out of the boat with him, for he couldn't walk or make his way home. Home he went with the man from the boat. He came to himself soon enough, for there was nothing wrong with him except that he had swallowed too much salt water.

'When he had recovered, in a day or two, he said to his wife that it was a fine, calm day, and that the best thing he could do was to go and catch a few connor fish for himself. His wife said he mustn't go, that perhaps the trouble of the other day would overtake him again. He said it wouldn't, for he would take good care of himself from that out, for he had bought his wisdom dearly.

'Off he went, and he had to go first to find bait for the fish. Crabs are the best bait, and they are to be found in holes at low tide. He started to hunt out the crabs, and he had collected a good lot, but in the end he put his hand into a hole where there were two crabs. When one of the crabs felt the hand in the hole, he gripped it, and as the hole was very narrow he couldn't withdraw his hand. He went black and red with terror, for the tide was flowing, and he couldn't run from it. At last the water was going into his mouth, and there would be little chance of his getting away soon. He gave one fierce pull at the hand at last. He preferred that to being suffocated, and he left the part of the hand that the crab had gripped in the hole. He made his way home, and he had lost nearly all his heart's blood by the time he reached the house.

'When his wife saw him coming towards her and the blood flowing, she fell to screaming, and asked what had taken his hand off him. He said there was nothing wrong with it, only if he had a rag he would twist it round the hand. She wouldn't give it to him, for fear he would go fishing. He snatched one of the children's shirts and wrapped it round the hand just as it was, and away round the hill with him to fish, with his hand tied up in the shirt.

'He went down to the sea, when he was a good way back along the hill, and he was soon catching plenty of connor fish, as fast as he could draw them up. After a time, when he had a fine row of them dead, he saw a great swell of sea rising away out from him, and he ran off as fast as he had it in his feet to go. And when he thought he was far enough up from the roller, he threw himself down to see how far the sea had come; and, as he looked, what should he see but the rod, the line, and the connor fish, and his old vest with a crown piece in the pocket, all the money he had in the world, afloat out on the sea. Every one of these things hurt him sorely, but worst of all was the old vest with the crown piece in its pocket. He was like that for a good space, sorrowful enough.

'And soon he saw coming towards him from the west a boat and it rowing fast. He went down some way to see would he recognize anybody in it. There were four oars to the boat, eight men in her and a woman at the stern. He didn't recognize a single soul of them at first, for they had their backs to him, but after a while some of them turned their faces in to land, and he knew the best part of them then. And he saw they were not people of this world, for the woman was his own sister who had died a few days ago. His feet and hands began to tremble when he saw who they were, all people who had passed from this world. He went up some way and hardly would his feet carry him up, though he was not a man easy to frighten before that.

'He stopped again, and said to himself that he would look again at the boat before going home. It was still in the same place when he turned round to go down. The captain rose up standing and spoke this verse that follows:

O rascal that never to Christ or the Virgin gave heed,
Or to God's holy Mass that the priest on a Sunday would read,
Death came to thy dear little sister and thou were not near,
And the tale of thine own end at last will be fearful to hear.

'He went home, and it was as much as the poor fellow could do. He was so terrified that he had nothing for his children when he came home, and, another thing that was troubling him greatly, his old vest was gone and his crown piece in it. When he reached the house he was sorrow-stricken and poverty-stricken into the bargain. The line and the rod and the old vest were the greater part of his property, and they were all clean gone from him then. He spent a week in the house without doing a thing.

'But one day a man from the village came in to sympathize with him, and asked him would he go killing seals with him. He leaped as light as a hound-puppy from the corner when he heard talk of the seals, for in those days they were a great addition to the people's livelihood, a thing they are not now. He went with them, and they made no stay till they reached the island in which they were most plentiful, Inisicíleáin. They went to the mouth of a cave, and there was a fair swell running. Two swimmers went in, and they needed another man to help to bring out

the seals they killed to the boat. They chose poor Donnchadh, and in he went. Each of them had a stick to kill the
seals with. Donnchadh killed one that had a young one
which she was suckling. They killed a fair share of seals in
the cave, but the day got worse with storm and swell, and
when they thought it time to drag the seals out on a rope,
they were afraid they wouldn't be able to win out themselves, not to mention the seals, the storm was so high.
One of them went out swimming, and had the end of the
rope with him. The second swimmer followed along the
rope. Poor Donnchadh had the other end of the rope in
the cave with him, and the two outside began to drag him
towards them. But before they could get him out the rope
broke, and away into the hole he went among the dead
seals, and he never came out again. The pair who got out
said that when Donnchadh was going to kill the seal with
the young one she spoke to him, and asked him not to kill
her till the young one should have drunk its enough of the
milk.'

As we came under the huge shelter of the Great Blasket
we lost the wind; they lowered the sail and took to the
oars, the eight oars going rapidly with the desire of home.
The tired dogs lay drowsing by the heap of dead rabbits,
and I sat lost in that half-trance that weariness and
hunger often bring in their train. The wind had moved
the pall of cloud, and through rifts and spaces in the west
the rays of the falling sun travelled over us and lighted
up the coasts of the bay. The mountain summits of Íbh
Ráthach were now clear of their long caps of cloud, and all
that world of hill and valley swam in the evening glow
counterchanged with fairy lights and shadows of dream.
Gulls and puffins and guillemots and all the lesser people
of the sea drifted or flew around us, and far out in the bay
the gannets were going home, flying high and straight, and

forgetting now to scan the water below them. No gannet, they say, ever comes to land on the Island or the rocks about it; they come in the morning from the Lesser Skellig, and with night return there to rest. The explanation of this is that the gannet, a royal bird, cannot rest on any rock which has not in it the nature of marble, and, since he is known to roost on the Skellig, we may conclude from this that the Skellig rock has in it something of the nature of marble; a truly medieval theory, proceeding from the explanation to the fact rather than in the modern fashion from the fact to the explanation. Now and again one of them would pass over the boat, and looking up I could see the yellow neck and black-rimmed eyes, and the beating of the long, slanted, sharply narrowing wings.

Soon we had turned the point of the Island, and slipped round the enclosing rock to the little harbour, and I stumbled stiffly up the road through the village to my evening meal, weary and hungry, and still dreaming of that lonely island of the sea haunted by fairies and ghostly memories, and the prayers of hermits so many centuries dead.

The Seal

THE little bay ringed round with broken cliffs
Gathers the tide-borne wrack,
And there the islanders come day by day
For weed that shall enrich their barren fields.
Here, since the cliff-path gaped,
Cloven by the winter's wrecking storms,
They had gathered to remake the shattered way.
We idled as they laboured
With listless, laughing talk of that and this,
When suddenly a seal,
Rising and falling on the changing tide,
Lifted a dripping face and looked at us,
A mournful face, more sad
Than the grey sadness of a moonlit wave.
We spoke, and in a moment it was gone,
And an unpeopled sea
Washed up and died in foam upon the shore.
Said one: 'He's lonely after his brother still.'
And so we heard the story,
A mournful memory of the Island, cherished
By the old dreaming people,
And told round the dim fire on winter nights.
One twilight of late spring
The men had killed a seal out on the beaches
And brought it to a sea-cave for the skinning,
And, as they worked red-handed,
A voice out of the sea called 'Brother!' once,
And then 'Brother!' again. Then silence, only
A wind that sighed on the unquiet sea.
So standing in the surf
They saw as now a seal rising and falling
On a slow swinging sea.
They lifted their red hands and he was gone
Silently slipping into a silent wave.

THE FAIRIES

AFTER supper I revived again, and drifted idly down, as was my habit, to Tomás's house in the lower village. Like all the older houses, it lies cosily tucked away under a bank of earth, and a stepped path leads down to it from the main roadway. As I came down the steps a blast of speech came through the open window, and I lifted the latch to find Tomás and his evening company engaged in heated argument. Silence fell as I pushed the door open. 'Prosperity from God on all here,' I said, entering, and, 'Long life to you' came the ritual answer, as I walked up the floor and took my seat by the fire.

Tomás was seated on the other side of the hearth, and opposite him, on the settle by the window, sat Maurice Eoghain Bháin, one of the O'Conors, a man of late middle-age, with prematurely whitened hair, his arms tightly folded, speaking in sudden jets with an abrupt and decisive impatience. On the table opposite him again sat two men, Peats Shéamuis, a little lively man, and another whose mysterious nickname is Caisht, one of the best fiddlers of the Island. They sat there, all leaning forward and with the air of fencers on guard, and you could almost see the words they had last spoken still carrying on the argument in the air between them.

'You were talking when I came in,' I said, 'and maybe there was some matter of argument between you.'

'You may say that, Bláheen,' cried Maurice, 'for here was Caisht saying that there are no such things as fairies and there never were.'

'No,' said Caisht, 'I am not saying that, maybe, there weren't fairies in the old time, but it is long since the priests got the upper hand of them, and there are no fairies in the

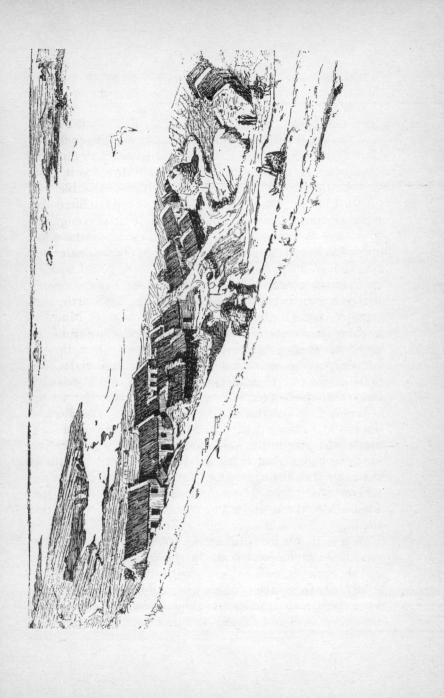

world to-day, nor for a long while now. What do you say, Bláheen?'

I was just collecting my words to answer when Peats Shéamuis broke in. 'Maybe there are fairies and maybe not,' he cried with an excited air, 'but everybody knows that there are things outside of this world, and they do things that no power in this world could do. And I know that for myself, for I have seen it with my own eyes.'

'Well,' I said, 'there was a wise man of the English in the old time, and he said that there are more things in heaven and earth than the learned can find any explanation for. But what have you seen with your own eyes that no power on earth could do?'

'Tell me now,' he said, 'would you believe that a church and a churchyard and all the bodies of the dead in it could be lifted in the air, and go four miles through the air, and be found the next day on a hillside four miles from the place where they started from?'

'Well, that would take a good deal of believing. But did you see the church and the churchyard and the bodies going through the air?'

'I did not. But this is how it happened. There was a church and a churchyard in Minard yonder up the bay, and a rich man in the neighbourhood used to be burying his dead there. And it irked him that the poor people of the place should be burying their dead in the same place where his relations were. And one day a poor man had been buried there, and a horse of the rich man's had died the day before, and what did he do but take his horse and bury it in that same churchyard. Nothing happened that day, but when they got up in the morning, the church wasn't there, nor the churchyard, nor the graves of the dead, only the grave of the horse. And they looked away from them, and what should they see but the church and the churchyard and the graves four miles away on the side of the hill, and they are there still, and I have seen them there with my own eyes. What do you say to that?'

'I don't know what to say,' I said. 'If you have seen them with your own eyes, there can be no doubt that there they are; but it is another matter what brought them there.'

'But did you ever hear the like of that tale happening in any part of the world?' asked Tomás.

'Well, it is a different story,' I said, 'but I have heard of a house vanishing from the middle of a great town in the neighbourhood of the City of London, though it wasn't the fairies or anything outside of the world that took it away.'

'Tell us the tale then.'

'It was this way it happened. A certain lady, an aunt of my wife's, had a house in a town that is called Norwood. And she was ill for some time, and at last the doctor said to her that she must travel for some months on the continent of Europe. So she sent her servants home, and shut up the house and went away, and she was away travelling for a quarter of the year. But at last her health came to her again, and she said to herself that she would go home to her fine house and be at ease in it. So home she went, and she came down the street where the house was, and when she came opposite the house, the house wasn't there, only the bare ground. She was amazed, and she stood looking at the place for a time till a neighbour came out and greeted her. And she said to the neighbour: "Where is my house?" and the neighbour said, "Didn't you send orders for it to be taken away?" And she said she had sent no such orders. Then the neighbour told the tale, how a man came up with a big lorry one day, and he went into the garden of the house, and set up a board in the garden, and on that board was written: "John Smith, Builder and Contractor", or some words like that. And the men went into the house and brought out the furniture, and put it on the lorry and carried it away. And they came back on the next day and the next after that, and so for a long time, and they took down the house brick by brick, till at last they had it all loaded up on the lorry and carried away. And then they took away the board, and nobody had seen them or the house since, or any trace of them. And neither they nor the house were ever seen again.'

'That is a strange story,' said Tomás, 'but it wasn't the fairies that took the house, nor any power outside the world, but evil men that were well schooled in the college of thievery.'

'You may say that,' said Maurice, 'for there are men well trained in that craft, too, and it is an easy life they have compared to the labour we have here, dragging a living out of the sea with our arms in the night, and often with no fish in the net at the end of it either.' And they fell to discussing the hard life of the poor, making a triple division of all mankind, the man with a post, the man earning daily pay, and the man under the mercy of the world.

'We are under the mercy of the world,' said one, 'and a poor mercy it is, hard living and little pay and the work-house and the grave at the end of it all. But the man that has a post can look the world in the face, and the man that works for his day's pay can always find some little thing to do and bring home money to his family at the day's end. And the sea is failing us now. Isn't it in the prophecy that the sea will be a dry cow a little before the world's end? And it will not be long now till the sea will be empty of fish, and wasn't that what the prophet meant when he said that she would be a dry cow?'

'Do you believe in the prophecy?' said another. 'There was an old man on the mainland, and he knew all the prophecies of Columcille, and Columcille said that a sign of the world's end would be a woman riding on a wheel, and when the first woman came round Slea Head riding a bicycle he came running into his house with terror in

his eyes, crying that the end of the world had come, for
he had seen a woman riding on a wheel, as it said in the
prophecy. And that is a long time ago now, and the world
hasn't ended yet.'

'Maybe that wasn't the woman and that wasn't the
wheel that the saint had in mind, and the prophecy will
come to pass yet.'

So we fell to discussing the world, how nobody knew when
the frame of things had come to be, and still less could any
say when it would come to an end; and one suggested that
it never would end, and another countered with the tradition of the saints, who had prophesied of the end of things
and the Judgement. And at last, by a turn in the discussion
which I have forgotten, we were back again among the
fairies, and Tomás was saying that there were cases, known
to everybody in that country-side, of women that had been
taken by the fairies to dwell with them in the liss.

'It is not so long ago,' he said, 'that a woman of my
mother's kin, the O'Sheas, was taken, and when I was
young I knew people who had seen her. She was a beautiful girl, and she hadn't been married a year when she fell
sick, and she said that she was going to die, and that if she
must die she would rather be in the home in which she had
spent her life than in a strange house where she had been
less than a year. So she went back to her mother's house,
and very soon she died and was buried. She hadn't been
buried more than a year when her husband married again,
and he had two children by his second wife. But one day
there came a letter to her people, a letter with a seal
on it.

'It was from a farmer who lived in the neighbourhood of
Fermoy. He said that now for some months, when the
family would go to bed at night in his farm, if any food
were left out they would find it gone in the morning. And

at last he said to himself that he would find out what it was
that came at night and took the food. So he sat up in a
corner of the kitchen one night, and in the middle of the
night the door opened and a woman came in, the most
beautiful woman he had ever seen with his eyes, and she
came up the kitchen and lifted the bowl of milk they had
left out, and drank of it. He came between her and the
door, and she turned to him and said that this was what
she had wanted. So he asked her who she was, and she
said that she came from the liss at the corner of his farm,
where the fairies kept her prisoner. They had carried her off
from a place in Ventry parish, and left a changeling in her
place, and the changeling had died and been buried in her
stead.

'She said that the farmer must write to her people and say
that she was in the liss with the fairies, and that she had
eaten none of the food of the fairies, for if once she ate of
their food she must remain with them for ever till she died;
and when she came near to death they would carry her
through the air and put her in the place of another young
woman, and carry the young woman back to be in the liss
with them in her stead. And when he wrote to her people,
he must ask her mother if she remembered one night
when her daughter lay sick, and the mother was sitting by
the fire, and, thinking so, she had forgotten everything
else, and the edge of her skirt had caught fire and was
burning for some time before she noticed it. If she remembered that night it would be a token for her, for on
that night her daughter had been carried off, and the
fire in her mother's skirt was the last thing she remembered of her life on earth. And when she had said this she
went out through the door, and the farmer saw her no
more.

'So the next day he wrote the letter as she had told him.
But her people did nothing, for they feared that if they

brought her back there would be trouble because of the new wife and her two children. And she came again and again to the farmer, and he wrote seven letters with seals, and the neighbours all said it was a shame to them to leave her with the fairies in the liss; and the husband said it was a great wrong to leave his wife in the liss, and, whatever trouble it would bring, they should go and fetch her out of the liss. So they set out, her own people and her husband, and when they had gone as far as Dingle, they said they would go and ask the advice of the priest.

'So they went to the priest that was there that time, and they told him the story from the beginning to the end. And when he had heard the story, he said that it was a hard case, and against the law of the church. And the husband said that, when they had brought the woman out of the liss, he would not bring her back with him to make scandal in the countryside, but would send her to America, and would live with his second wife and her children. But the priest said that even if a man's wife were in America, she was still his wife, and it was against the law of the Pope that a man should have two wives; and, though it was a hard thing, they must leave her in the liss with the fairies, for it was a less evil that she should eat the fairy bread and be always with the fairies in the liss than that God's law should be broken and a man have two wives living in this world.

'They found nothing to say against the priest, and they went back home sorrowing. And when the woman heard this from the farmer she went back with the fairies to the liss, and ate their bread and remained with them.'

This tale loosened the lips of the company, and one after another they spoke of like happenings, and how in one year the fairies took fifteen young women from one parish, and none of them had ever come back. But now the power of the priests was so strong that the fairies were mastered and their magic gone from them.

It was now late, and I was falling asleep in my chair after a long day under the open sky. I rose, and, going down the kitchen, turned in the doorway to say 'Goodnight.' 'A lucky night to you,' they answered as one man, and I went out into a night of stars. For the wind had now swept the sky clear of the last wisps of cloud, and in that cold, lucid air of early spring the innumerable company of the stars glittered and crackled above the sleeping village.

Climbing the uneven path to the upper village, I went a little way from the houses and looked out over the sea. The flowing line of the coast of Ireland was dimly visible across the sound, Beiginis and the Rocks of the Road floated blackly in a hueless sea, and life seemed to have withdrawn into the vast arch of the sky, poised in the west on the Atlantic horizon, and based upon the other hand on the shadowy mountains beyond the farthest inlet of Dingle Bay.

It is no doubt a personal fancy, but often on such frosty, mistless nights, I have imagined in the palpitating radiance of the nearer constellations and the clustering glow of the Milky Way—the Way of Saint James the pilgrim Middle Ages called it, as though reconciling something pagan to the faith—a conscious life indifferent or inimical to man. In such a mood and under such a sky it is easy to believe in the reality of the fairies, and it may be that such moods and such skies of night first gave them birth; that from the cold lunar rays and the restless sparkle of the stars imagination bodied forth figures and allegories of its own fears, and gave them a being and a habitation on the earth, and at last a power upon the bodies and the minds of men. They are an image of man's unreconciled distrust of nature, and it was in the cities, which have devised a thousand ways of dissembling natural needs and natural fears, that men began to forget them.

Here, too, they will be gone in a few short years, I thought, for they have for a habitation the minds of the old men and women, and the young people no longer believe in them. And I left these thoughts, and the cold, clear night that had given them birth, and forgot the weariness of the long day in a dreamless slumber on the birds' feathers which I had left so hastily in the early morning.

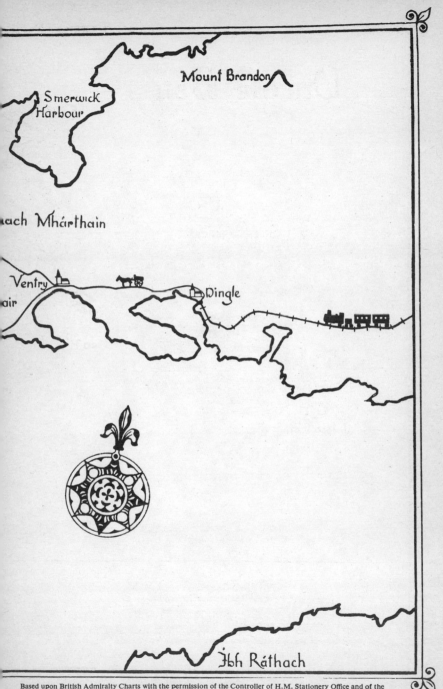

Mount Brandon

Smerwick Harbour

ach Mhárthain

Ventry

air

Dingle

Ibh Ráthach

Based upon British Admiralty Charts with the permission of the Controller of H.M. Stationery Office and of the Hydrographer of the Navy

OXFORD

MORE OXFORD PAPERBACKS

Details of a selection of other Oxford Paperbacks follow. A complete list of Oxford Paperbacks, including The World's Classics, Twentieth-Century Classics, OPUS, Past Masters, Oxford Authors, Oxford Shakespeare, and Oxford Paperback Reference, is available in the UK from the General Publicity Department, Oxford University Press (RS), Walton Street, Oxford, OX2 6DP.

In the USA, complete lists are available from the Paperbacks Marketing Manager, Oxford University Press, 200 Madison Avenue, New York, NY 10016.

Oxford Paperbacks are available from all good bookshops. In case of difficulty, customers in the UK can order direct from Oxford University Press Bookshop, 116 High Street, Oxford, Freepost, OX1 4BR, enclosing full payment. Please add 10 per cent of the published price for postage and packing.

SCIENCE IN OXFORD PAPERBACKS

Oxford Paperbacks offers a challenging and controversial list of science and mathematics books, ranging from theories of evolution to analyses of the latest micro-technology, from studies of the nervous system to advice on teenage health.

THE AGES OF GAIA

A Biography of Our Living Earth

James Lovelock

In his first book, *Gaia: A New Look at Life on Earth* (OPB, 1982), James Lovelock proposed a startling new theory of life. Previously it was accepted that plants and animals evolve on, but are distinct from, an inanimate planet. Gaia maintained that the Earth, its rocks, oceans, and atmosphere, and all living things are part of one great organism, evolving over the vast span of geological time. Much scientific work has since confirmed Lovelock's ideas.

In this new book, Lovelock elaborates the basis of a new and unified view of the earth and life sciences, discussing recent scientific developments in detail: the greenhouse effect, acid rain, the depletion of the ozone layer and the effects of ultraviolet radiation, the emission of CFCs, and nuclear power. He demonstrates the geophysical interaction of atmosphere, oceans, climate, and the Earth's crust, regulated comfortably for life by living organisms using the energy of the sun.

'Open the cover and bathe in great draughts of air that excitingly argue the case that "the earth is alive".' David Bellamy, *Observer*

'Lovelock deserves to be described as a genius.' *New Scientist*

'He is to science what Gandhi was to politics.' Fred Pearce, *New Scientist*

Also in Oxford Paperbacks:

What is Ecology?   Denis Owen
The Selfish Gene 2/e   Richard Dawkins
The Sacred Beetle and Other Great Essays in Science
Chosen and introduced by Martin Gardner

SCIENCE IN OXFORD PAPERBACKS

Oxford Paperbacks' expanding science and mathematics list offers a range of books across the scientific spectrum by men and women at the forefront of their fields, including Richard Dawkins, Martin Gardner, James Lovelock, Raymond Smullyan, and Nobel Prize winners Peter Medawar and Gerald Edelman.

THE SELFISH GENE
Second Edition
Richard Dawkins

Our genes made us. We animals exist for their preservation and are nothing more than their throwaway survival machines. The world of the selfish gene is one of savage competition, ruthless exploitation, and deceit. But what of the acts of apparent altruism found in nature—the bees who commit suicide when they sting to protect the hive, or the birds who risk their lives to warn the flock of an approaching hawk? Do they contravene the fundamental law of gene selfishness? By no means: Dawkins shows that the selfish gene is also the subtle gene. And he holds out the hope that our species—alone on earth—has the power to rebel against the designs of the selfish gene. This book is a call to arms. It is both manual and manifesto, and it grips like a thriller.

The Selfish Gene, Richard Dawkins's brilliant first book and still his most famous, is an international bestseller in thirteen languages. For this greatly expanded edition, endnotes have been added, giving fascinating reflections on the original text, and there are two major new chapters.

'learned, witty, and very well written . . . exhilaratingly good.' Sir Peter Medawar, *Spectator*

'Who should read this book? Everyone interested in the universe and their place in it.' Jeffrey R. Baylis, *Animal Behaviour*

'the sort of popular science writing that makes the reader feel like a genius' *New York Times*

Also in Oxford Paperbacks:

The Extended Phenotype   Richard Dawkins
The Ages of Gaia   James Lovelock
The Unheeded Cry   Bernard E. Rollin

MEDICINE IN OXFORD PAPERBACKS

Oxford Paperbacks offers an increasing list of medical studies and reference books of interest to the specialist and general reader alike, including The Facts series, authoritative and practical guides to a wide range of common diseases and conditions.

CONCISE MEDICAL DICTIONARY
Third Edition

Written without the use of unnecessary technical jargon, this illustrated medical dictionary will be welcomed as a home reference, as well as an indispensible aid for all those working in the medical profession.

Nearly 10,000 important terms and concepts are explained, including all the major medical and surgical specialities, such as gynaecology and obstetrics, paediatrics, dermatology, neurology, cardiology, and tropical medicine. This third edition contains much new material on pre-natal diagnosis, infertility treatment, nuclear medicine, community health, and immunology. Terms relating to advances in molecular biology and genetic engineering have been added, and recently developed drugs in clinical use are included. A feature of the dictionary is its unusually full coverage of the fields of community health, psychology, and psychiatry.

Each entry contains a straightforward definition, followed by a more detailed description, while an extensive crossreference system provides the reader with a comprehensive view of a particular subject.

Also in Oxford Paperbacks:

Drugs and Medicine   Roderick Cawson and Roy Spector
Travellers' Health: How to Stay Healthy Abroad 2/e
Richard Dawood
I'm a Health Freak Too!
Aidan Macfarlane and Ann McPherson
Problem Drinking   Nick Heather and Ian Robertson

WOMEN'S STUDIES FROM
OXFORD PAPERBACKS

Ranging from the *A–Z of Women's Health* to *Wayward Women: A Guide to Women Travellers*, Oxford Paperbacks cover a wide variety of social, medical, historical, and literary topics of particular interest to women.

DESTINED TO BE WIVES
The Sisters of Beatrice Webb
Barbara Caine

Drawing on their letters and diaries, Barbara Caine's fascinating account of the lives of Beatrice Webb and her sisters, the Potters, presents a vivid picture of the extraordinary conflicts and tragedies taking place behind the respectable façade which has traditionally characterized Victorian and Edwardian family life.

The tensions and pressures of family life, particularly for women; the suicide of one sister; the death of another, probably as a result of taking cocaine after a family breakdown; the shock felt by the older sisters at the promiscuity of their younger sister after the death of her husband are all vividly recounted. In all the crises they faced, the sisters formed the main network of support for each other, recognizing that the 'sisterhood' provided the only security in a society which made women subordinate to men, socially, legally, and economically.

Other women's studies titles:

A–Z of Women's Health   Derek Llewellyn-Jones
'Victorian Sex Goddess': Lady Colin Campbell and the Sensational Divorce Case of 1886   G. H. Fleming
Wayward Women: A Guide to Women Travellers
Jane Robinson
Catherine the Great: Life and Legend   John T. Alexander

OXFORD LIVES

Biography at its best—this popular series offers authoritative accounts of the lives of famous men and women from the arts and sciences, politics and exploration.

'SUBTLE IS THE LORD'

The Science and the Life of Albert Einstein

Abraham Pais

Abraham Pais, an award-winning physicist who knew Einstein personally during the last nine years of his life, presents a guide to the life and the thought of the most famous scientist of our century. Using previously unpublished papers and personal recollections from their years of acquaintance, the narrative illuminates the man through his work with both liveliness and precision, making this *the* authoritative scientific biography of Einstein.

'The definitive life of Einstein.'
Brian Pippard, *Times Literary Supplement*

'By far the most important study of both the man and the scientist.' Paul Davies, *New Scientist*

'An outstanding biography of Albert Einstein that one finds oneself reading with sheer pleasure.' *Physics Today*

Also in the Oxford Lives series:

Peter Fleming: A Biography   Duff Hart-Davies
Gustav Holst: A Biography   Imogen Holst
T. H. White   Sylvia Townsend Warner
Joyce Cary: Gentleman Rider   Alan Bishop